EUGENE H. PE
Translator of THE**MESS**

EVERY STEP
AN ARRIVAL

A 90-DAY DEVOTIONAL
FOR EXPLORING GOD'S WORD

WATERBROOK

EVERY STEP AN ARRIVAL

Hardcover ISBN 978-1-60142-973-5
eBook ISBN 978-1-60142-974-2

Cover design by Kristopher K. Orr
Cover illustration by Alexey Kurbatov

Library of Congress Cataloging-in-Publication Data
Names: Peterson, Eugene H., 1932- author.
Title: Every step an arrival : a 90-day devotional for exploring God's word / Eugene H. Peterson.
Description: First Edition. | Colorado Springs : WaterBrook, 2018.
Identifiers: LCCN 2018002999| ISBN 9781601429735 (hardcover) | ISBN 9781601429742 (electronic)
Subjects: LCSH: Bible—Meditations.
Classification: LCC BS491.5 .P46 2018 | DDC 242/.5—dc23
LC record available at https://lccn.loc.gov/2018002999

Printed in the United States of America
2018—First Edition

10 9 8 7 6 5 4 3 2 1

SPECIAL SALES
Most WaterBrook books are available at special quantity discounts when purchased in bulk by corporations, organizations, and special-interest groups. Custom imprinting or excerpting can also be done to fit special needs. For information, please email specialmarketscms@penguinrandomhouse.com or call 1-800-603-7051.

CONTENTS

LETTER TO THE READER

Dear Reader,

Eugene Peterson has long loved Denise Levertov's poem "Overland to the Islands." The poet conjures up the image of a dog moving "intently haphazard," sniffing and dancing over rocks and mud, disdaining nothing his nose registers along the way. But the dog has a trick afoot, which is that he always

> keeps moving, changing
> pace and approach but
> not direction—"every step an arrival."*

At first glance, the words, thoughts, and phrases we've curated from Eugene Peterson's library of sermons may have a very intently haphazard feel. One devotion doesn't logically follow the next, and there's no thematic thread sewn clearly through each entry. Peterson would say something like, "Welcome to the spiritual life." An organized approach is never the goal but rather a wide-eyed curiosity that disdains nothing and is willing to sniff out anything

---

* Denise Levertov, *Selected Poems* (New York: New Directions, 2002), 7.

that captures the attention. Living a life with such discipline indeed makes every step an arrival.

We hope you'll allow these scriptures and thoughts to take your mind and heart wherever they may go. You never know what the Spirit will use to encourage or challenge or humble or comfort. But don't forget the dog's trick—to keep moving—because it will serve you well over the next ninety days.

Two final things. The devotions lend themselves to shedding light on your life or on God's nature. Obviously at times these two areas dovetail, but keeping the distinction in mind can be helpful. In addition, each entry is followed by a pause of sorts—sometimes a question, sometimes a reflection. You could even use the words there to form your own prayer for the day, certainly not as an ending point but rather as a beginning for the arrivals that await you.

Sincerely,
WaterBrook and Multnomah Editorial Team

The Contrast of Darkness and Light

God created the Heavens and Earth—all you see, all you don't see. Earth was a soup of nothingness, a bottomless emptiness, an inky blackness. God's Spirit brooded like a bird above the watery abyss.

God spoke: "Light!"

And light appeared.

—Genesis 1:1–3

There is significance in the first day's creative act: God said, "Light!" And light appeared. The universe is established with God's light shining through everything. There is a profound understanding of this in the way in which a day is described in Genesis and subsequently in all Jewish life. "There was evening and there was morning, one day" (verse 5, RSV). An odd way to describe a day, but not if you see it as a victory of God's light. *Evening* has the sense, in Hebrew, of termination, bringing to a conclusion. A day is described first as the conclusion of the creative work of God, then night, a time of sleep, the incursion of darkness, a threat to the order of creation, a sign of chaos to come. Does night or light have the last word? The answer is in the phrase "and there was morning, one day."

Morning in Hebrew has the meaning of "penetration."* God's day is not complete until light shines again, penetrating the darkness and dispersing the shadows. The creative action of God is light, which encloses and limits a temporary darkness. All that we see as a threat to God's creative action is held in check and controlled by his light. The shadows are there—night descends upon life—and there is that which seems to defy God, to disturb his order and his purpose: sickness, death, trouble, and sorrow. But it does not have the last word: "And there was morning, one day."

Identify an area of your life in which you need God's light to penetrate the dimness. Will night or light have the last word? Talk with God about the clarity you seek.

---

* Strong's Concordance, s.v. "boqer: morning," http://biblehub.com/hebrew/1242.htm.

The Best Start in Understanding Ourselves

God created human beings;
   he created them godlike,
Reflecting God's nature.
   He created them male and female.
God blessed them:
   "Prosper! Reproduce! Fill Earth! Take
      charge!
Be responsible for fish in the sea and
      birds in the air,
   for every living thing that moves on
      the face of Earth."

—Genesis 1:27-28

When we Christians want to understand ourselves accurately and deeply, we don't put ourselves in front of a mirror. Persons who stand before mirrors are not famous for the accuracy or depth of their self-understanding. Friends can give valuable insight, but each insight is only a fragment of the reality. When we want to sharpen and deepen self-understanding, we look at Adam.

I hope when I pronounce the name *Adam* you will not think of a nude figure strolling through a semitropical garden with flowers woven through his hair, murmuring small talk with lions and parakeets, and plucking an occasional pomegranate for a snack. No, Adam is you. Adam is the point at which our self-understanding begins. The Bible does not describe the anatomy of Adam; it does not discuss the psychology of Adam; it does not give us the history of Adam. In those respects, Adam is a great mystery. What we get are a few lines that set forth the meaning of Adam. We discover in him the essentials of what it means to be a human being: we are a result of God's creative work, we are created to be in relation with other people, and we are responsible for the world around us.

Often our confusion about the world begins with a lack of clarity regarding who we are. Who are you in relation to others, in relation to God, and in relation to the world? Ask God to make clear to you who he made you to be and what it means to be fully human in his eyes.

Our Faithful God
Is Changeless

Until you return to that ground yourself,
    dead and buried;
    you started out as dirt, you'll end up dirt.

—Genesis 3:19

We desperately need this reminder. It sounds just a bit archaic and is denied by many present circumstances. We are constantly reminded and inevitably impressed with our power. We can do nearly anything we want. No longer bound to the cycles of the seasons, we create our own heat in winter and cold in summer. No longer restricted by the natural rhythms of night and day, we produce our own light and work where we will. We are born in immaculate, germ-free hospitals; grow up in controlled, managed environments; and live our lives dominated by machines, gadgets, inventions, and constructions. We are not dependent on God's creation and scarcely give it a thought, and then only on vacation.

Meanwhile, a tragic thing has happened to us: we've grown fearful. And panic follows terror and leaves a legacy of anxiety that has become the permanent spiritual characteristic of our age. Our times are marked by spiritual disorientation and a haunting soullessness. It is not easy to remember that we are dust, even if we want to. So what do we do?

Here is a single and concrete suggestion: pray a penitential prayer. Psalm 102 is a good place to begin. Read it aloud, start to finish. Remember that you are dust. And remember that the Lord is "enthroned for ever; [his] name endures to all generations" (verse 12, RSV).

Awakened by restlessness in the night, we fail to shut out our fears. We are taken to our most vulnerable place, the place where we acknowledge we have no control over our destiny. Release your vulnerabilities and fears to God as you pray through Psalm 102.

Unexpected Evidence of God's Love

GOD told him, "No. Anyone who kills Cain will pay for it seven times over." GOD put a mark on Cain to protect him so that no one who met him would kill him.

Cain left the presence of GOD and lived in No-Man's-Land, east of Eden.

—Genesis 4:15–16

The natural course of sin is damnation and death. Left to itself, it avalanches to its own destruction. Resentment breeds resentment, greed begets greed, anger causes anger, lust provokes lust, reprisals ignite worse reprisals, and deceit is matched by deceit. The cycle of sin spirals, increasing in intensity and rushing to destroy itself by its own acts. Anybody can see that, and everybody experiences it.

But then God breaks the cycle. He intervenes in this relentless, compulsive, cause-effect sequence with "Not so!" God does this divinely creative act, placing a mark of his redeeming love on man the sinner so that there is an opportunity to respond to love and grace. Cain was not relieved of the loneliness, the wandering, and the sense of loss that followed his murdering his brother. But he was able to go to a new place and found a city and became ancestor to a series of creative giants. The mark God placed on him enabled him to live beyond the guilt and judgment he well deserved but God did not permit. Cain carried with him the consequences of his sin, but he did not carry God's continuing anger. It was just the opposite: Cain was marked with the sign of God's protective care.

Think about the ways you are living with the consequences of things you have done and said. Ask God to help you make amends, to make restitution to those you have wronged. As you do this, ask him to show you the marks of his love placed on you.

God Is Not a Problem Solver On Call

GOD did to Sarah what he promised: Sarah became pregnant and gave Abraham a son in his old age, and at the very time God had set. Abraham named him Isaac.

—Genesis 21:2–3

As simple as they are, birth stories do some things for persons of faith that need doing over and over and over again, for our tendency is to do one of two things with God. One is to flatten him down into the banal and the humdrum. We lose all sense of mystery. We reduce him to morals or platitudes or a genial source of good advice. We lose all sense of the transcendent or the glorious or the beyond. The other tendency is to sentimentalize God into diversion or entertainment. We fantasize him and hope for an escape from whatever we don't like about what is happening to us at the time. Most of us do one of these two things alternately, yet our lives are unchanged.

The message of the gospel is that God invades us with new

life, and the life changes what we presently are. He is not a means by which we solve problems. He is not a means to avoid problems. He creates new life. He is not a problem solver but a person creator. These birth stories are all around you—in the person of your child or your wife or your husband or your friend or your parent or your brother or your sister or your neighbor. Be observant. Be aware.

God is "not a problem solver but a person creator." Have you viewed God as a means to an end, a divine solution to problems rather than a Creator who walks with you through life? Ask him to birth a holy awe in your life.

Roadblocks Mean Nothing to God

I'll bless you—oh, how I'll bless you! And I'll make sure that your children flourish—like stars in the sky! like sand on the beaches! And your descendants will defeat their enemies. All nations on Earth will find themselves blessed through your descendants because you obeyed me.

—Genesis 22:17-18

This is not a story about Abraham, a hero of the faith who survived all odds to become the father of the Hebrew nation. Abraham is only the person in whom the election and promise of God achieve visibility and historical verification. We are always making human-interest stories out of biblical characters, trying to extract some moral that we can imitate. But it is a waste of time for the most part. There is so little to imitate. Only a couple of incidents in Abraham's life are worthy of imitation, and not being sheepherders in the Middle Bronze Age, we are not capable of reliving them anyway. No, this is a story about God's choice of man (of us!) and how he resourcefully and masterfully completes his purpose despite every roadblock, every diversion, every sin, and all unbelief. It is the story about God's choice of you and how he successfully executes his will in you.

At the same time there is something we can do. Even though we are not at the center of the stage, we are not merely spectators. The great thing that Abraham did was he "believed the LORD; and [the LORD] reckoned it to him as righteousness" (Genesis 15:6, RSV). This we can do as well.

God chose to work out his will on earth through humanity. That means he chose you to be part of the process. Join Abraham in believing God's promise.

Resurrection Faith in Song

Moses and the Israelites sang this song to
GOD, giving voice together,
I'm singing my heart out to GOD—what a
victory!
He pitched horse and rider into the
sea.

—Exodus 15:1

The Song of Moses is a case study in response. Singing is what people do when they believe in what God has done. It's the most expressive way in which we make known our faith. It catches up not only our minds but also our emotions, puts our bodies into operation, so that as a whole we give expression to what we believe. The Song of Moses is obviously a resurrection faith directed to God. Resurrection faith is directed to God. It knows that God has made the difference. It realizes the impact of God on our lives.

The characteristic form of writing for Egypt, for Babylonia, for Assyria, for the Hittites—all these neighboring nations—was not a song but an enemies list, a compilation of all the kings they had killed, the armies they had vanquished, and the cities they had devastated. The result was long, interminable, dull statistics. That's often the way men react to the reality of victory when they believe they are in charge. All they can do is gather data and make statistics out of it. The Hebrews did something very different. They sang a song, packed with exact and vivid metaphors: "The horse and his rider he has thrown into the sea" (RSV). Rather than regurgitating data, the Hebrews revel in exact detail. Rather than compiling a boring list for the reader, the Hebrews invite us into something set in motion, something going forward: a song.

Rather than keeping a ledger of defeated enemies, God's ancient people voiced their resurrection faith in song to him. Name one way God has made a difference in your life. Now tell the story back to him in the spirit of song.

Moving Aside to Give God Room

GOD said to Moses, "Climb higher up the mountain and wait there for me; I'll give you tablets of stone, the teachings and commandments that I've written to instruct them."

—Exodus 24:12

The picture of Moses in Exodus 24 shows him at the pinnacle. The deliverance from Egypt has been accomplished; God's will is revealed to the people. Moses is the leader of the people; Moses is the spokesman for God. He is the key person in the people's relation with God; he is the key person in God's relation with the people. It would seem natural on the basis of this to conclude that Moses is an indispensable person—worthy of complete honor, entitled to special treatment. But Moses is portrayed to us only as necessary, not indispensable. If Moses had not done it, God would have prepared another. The great thing in the story is not what Moses did but what God did. God calls; God gives; God instructs. All that is significant in Moses is that he went at God's call and waited for his word.

Moses is important because he knew how to get out of the way so God could be in the way. Moses disappeared in the cloud. He stayed, hidden, on the mountain for forty days and nights. When Moses did reappear, he gave the people God's word. He didn't tell the exciting story of his forty days on the mountain. He did not show a set of slides of the views from Sinai. He was absolutely silent about himself in order that he might talk about God. The projection of personality in matters of religion is always a manifestation of pride and a form of disease in the gospel. We come to a place of worship to find out about God, not about man. We are here to get ourselves in relation with God, not to be entertained with religious tales of the saints and sinners.

God is the center of the story. One after another, the heroes of faith stepped aside to give him his rightful place. Think about what it takes to step aside, to get out of the way to allow God his rightful place in your life.

Begging for an Idol

When the people realized that Moses was taking forever in coming down off the mountain, they rallied around Aaron and said, "Do something. Make gods for us who will lead us. That Moses, the man who got us out of Egypt—who knows what's happened to him?"

—Exodus 32:1

They knew they had been set free; they had all shared that experience—it was incontestable. They were now going to learn to live in relation to the vast but invisible reality of God. But day succeeded day, and there was nothing but emptiness. Moses was gone, and the people began to make demands: "We are tired of waiting. We are tired of nothing. We want something. Make us gods." So Aaron made them a golden calf. At that moment, Aaron ceased being a leader and became an accomplice.

We are always looking for a religion that has no demands, only rewards—a religion that bedazzles and entertains, in which there is no waiting and no emptiness. And we can usually find someone around who will help us make up some sort of a golden calf. In a moment of boredom, we turn our backs on the love of God.

We abandon the awesome stillness of worship and fill the air with third-rate jingles. We get tired of participating in the strenuous life of freedom and of faith, and we regress to the old slave religion that reduces God to a decoration or an amulet.

And God's wrath is stirred. It is not an anger that intends to destroy but one that provokes and stimulates the work of petition: prayers for mercy and cries for compassion. The mercy will not eliminate the judgment, but God will never abandon his people.

Think about a time of waiting, when God failed to make himself known, when you were left in silence and seemingly alone. What did you learn about yourself, God, and the reality of faith?

What Really Happens in the Desert

Gather from among you an offering for GOD. Receive on GOD's behalf what everyone is willing to give as an offering.

—Exodus 35:5

The parallel isn't exact, but by shifting a few details, we ought to be able to see ourselves in that desert. Even though we are a people of considerable means, very few of us are millionaires. We probably all consider ourselves economically in a kind of slave status—serving the bank, the mortgage company, the college-loan-repayment collector, and a series of retailers. Some of us make an honest salary, but it is spoken for before we even get it home. We usually finish the month as poor as we began it. We may dream of the land of Canaan flowing with milk and honey, out there somewhere in the future, but right now we are in the desert.

Had Moses been a professional fund-raiser, surely he would have taken a look at the Hebrew people and declared one word: *poverty*. But Moses was a servant who knew that each person had been graciously and miraculously given a free life by God's deliverance. In other words, he knew the people had a generous heart. It was on that basis that he made his appeal. He didn't say, "Everyone who managed to salvage something from Egypt" or "Everyone in a special income bracket" or "Everyone who wants to get God's attention by contributing to a worthy cause." No, Moses said, "Everyone with a generous heart" (see RSV). Moses knew the only lasting basis for giving is gratitude.

Much of life requires earning: a salary, a place on the team, a scholarship, a raise, a promotion. God is the opposite of the world's system. You received his grace and mercy as a result of his generosity. When you give freely, you are living according to his system.

Serving God Involves Being Served by Him

He erected the Courtyard all around The Dwelling and the Altar, and put up the screen for the Courtyard entrance.

Moses finished the work.

The Cloud covered the Tent of Meeting, and the Glory of GOD filled The Dwelling.

—Exodus 40:33–34

All the depth and profundity of worship is summarized in those last two sentences. *Moses finished the work*—that is, the service that man brings to God; that is, the material and physical work of building, planning, searching out, thinking, and doing. Energy is expended, calluses build up on hands, muscles are tired, discouragements are surmounted, determination finds a way, sacrifices are made, a tabernacle is built.

The Cloud covered the Tent of Meeting, and the Glory of God filled The Dwelling—that is, the service that God brings to man; that is, the Spirit of God invading our hearts with his healing, restoring, redeeming, renewing presence. Love is released, knowledge is shed abroad, peace is infused, and grace is lavished.

All true worship has this deep, rhythmic movement of man's service to God and God's service to man. Man builds a tent, and God fills it with his glory. Man constructs a church; God's cloud of providence covers it.

This is no quid pro quo, this rhythm of our service to God and God's service to us. It is not a matter of his rewarding our worthiness or our hard work. It is rather the rhythm of life in God's system. He gives, we give, he gives more, and we respond in gratitude. This is part of the beauty that God brings to our lives.

Defilement and Damnation

> When Aaron finishes making atonement for the
> Holy of Holies, the Tent of Meeting, and the Altar,
> he will bring up the live goat, lay both hands on
> the live goat's head, and confess all the iniqui-
> ties of the People of Israel, all their acts of rebel-
> lion, all their sins.
>
> —Leviticus 16:20–21

S in does two things to a person: it defiles him and destines him
to judgment. It dirties a soul, and it damns it. A sinner reflecting on his sin is unhappy about the messiness, the aimlessness,
the squalid interior of his life. He is also, if he is at all perceptive,
anxious about the consequences—the judgment he has let himself
in for.

If sin does two things to a person, atonement must counter
them both. To be effective, it must deal with defilement and damnation. In the Hebrew ritual, the goat for the Lord was slain, and
its blood cleansed the defilement; the scapegoat took care of the
consequences. Imagine the relief, the lightness of the Hebrews as
they watched the scapegoat, their sins heaped on his head, driven
out to the edges of the desert to Azazel. Let that old desert demon

Azazel have him. Drive the sins to the hot, inhuman desert sands. The merciless, stinging desert wind would take care of their sins. They would never again dog Israel.

Imagine the cleansing, the sense of new life as the blood of the Lord's goat was shed for the Hebrews' sins. They were in fellowship with their God now. The enmity was gone, the relation purified. They could sing the song of the redeemed.

Defilement is what sin does to us; damnation is what sin introduces as our eternal end. Except for God's intervention. We have needs, and God addresses our needs. Even our sin, the most destructive reality of life—and the most foreign to God's character—is met and overwhelmed by his coming to us.

Saying Right While Doing Wrong

Balak said to Balaam, "What's this? I brought you here to curse my enemies, and all you've done is bless them."

—Numbers 23:11

The Jews had been moving from their Egyptian bondage to a conquest of the Promised Land and amassing a series of impressive victories along the way. There was a rumor that all this was because God was on their side. They were almost to the point of their entry into Canaan when they had one last group to get through. And Balak was the enemies' king. You have to give him credit. Nobody seemed to be making headway against the Jews using military force, so he concluded that if an army could not defeat the Jews, maybe a pagan prophet could. If he could get Balaam on his side, get him to pronounce a curse on the Jews, then that would be the way to stop them. Balaam was enough of a prophet to know he shouldn't do it, but the offer of a large sum of money was too great.

So, a warning against religious eloquence—your own or someone else's. Balaam had a great reputation as a man of God, but it was all external. His oratory was all in his mouth, not his heart. He had nothing inside. He was a hollow man. What he really wanted to do was please whoever was paying him or admiring him. Balaam said all the right things but did all the wrong things.

It is one of the easiest styles for Christians to pick up, this learning to sound righteous and then letting the sounds substitute for a life of obedience to God.

"With the tongue we praise our Lord and Father, and with it we curse human beings, who have been made in God's likeness" (James 3:9, NIV). God said through Isaiah that his people were honoring him with their lips while their hearts were far from him (see Isaiah 29:13). Ask God to reveal your heart to you.

The Messiah Is Light and Power

He spoke his oracle-message:
>   Decree of Balaam son of Beor,
>   decree of the man with 20/20 vision,
>   Decree of the man who hears godly
>   speech,
>   who knows what's going on with the
>   High God,
>   Who sees what The Strong God reveals,
>   who bows in worship and sees what's
>   real.

—Numbers 24:15–16

Balaam—that ancient, pagan prophet who fell to his knees before the presence of God and thus was prevented from seeing anything around him before having his eyes uncovered in a vision of God Almighty:

I see him, but not right now,
   I perceive him, but not right here;

A star rises from Jacob

    a scepter from Israel. (verse 17)

He described himself as "the man with 20/20 vision," as if his previous life was lived in a religious fog and mist. Then suddenly the mist dispersed, and in the clear light of day he saw God's purposes. What he saw in his vision was the Messiah, the Christ, God in human flesh working out his salvation in the stuff of history. His vision was still well over a thousand years before the actual event, yet it was seen clearly. Looking down the long vistas of history, remote yet cleanly outlined against the horizon, he saw what God would finally do.

Balaam used two images to describe what he saw: a star would come forth out of Jacob, and a scepter would rise out of Israel. The star was a representation of light, the scepter a representation of power. Light and power—the two symbols that would come to full expression in the life of Jesus Christ.

In a vision, Balaam was shown symbols of light and power, pointing to the coming Messiah. How has Jesus appeared in your life as a presence of light and/or power?

Forgiving Disobedience, Renewing Life

You saw with your own eyes what GOD did at Baal Peor, how GOD destroyed from among you every man who joined in the Baal Peor orgies. But you, the ones who held tight to GOD, your God, are alive and well, every one of you, today.

—Deuteronomy 4:3–4

You can look back over your lifetime, search through family histories, observe the traditions of the nation, and see what happens when a person declines to respond to God, rejects the living presence of his love, refuses to deal with the mercy of God, and rebels against his counsel. It is all written down in history books and family legends, and the sum total is that it doesn't work. But the positive evidence is, if possible, even more striking: "You, the ones who held tight to GOD, your God, are alive and well, every one of you, today" (verse 4). The very fact that you are alive and not dead, breathing oxygen and not moldering in the grave, able to feel joy or guilt, experience peace or anxiety or worry or trust—that is overwhelming evidence for trust in God and obedience to him.

Disobedience is a learning disability that is fairly easy to diagnose. Among the usual symptoms are sluggish moral reflexes, an uneasy conscience that interferes with your digestion, a load of guilt that makes you tire easily, and a low-grade depression that saps you of creative energies. For you who recognize such symptoms in yourself I have good news: God loves you, and he is ready to forgive your sins and create new and eternal life in you. God is ready, at this moment, to cancel out the past, to wipe out the record, to burn the files on you. Nothing you have done or can imagine disqualifies you from accepting what he is even now doing for you.

What are the symptoms of your own disobedience to God? What prevents you from approaching him for forgiveness and asking him to cancel your past and restore your relationship?

God Links Your Past, Present, and Future

Yes, it was you—your eyes—that saw every great thing that GOD did.

So it's you who are in charge of keeping the entire commandment that I command you today so that you'll have the strength to invade and possess the land that you are crossing the river to make your own. Your obedience will give you a long life on the soil that GOD promised to give your ancestors and their children, a land flowing with milk and honey.

—Deuteronomy 11:7–9

Deuteronomic education is the expansion of life in two directions: into the past and into the future. It puts you in active relationship with the energies of the past and the future. The whole task of Christian commitment is to weld a connection between God's past and God's future in your personal history. Your faith takes the remembered past and the expected future and fuses them together in your personality. American historian Henry Adams once said that "nothing in education is so astonishing as

the amount of ignorance it accumulates in the form of inert facts."
The goal of God's education is that there be no inert facts at all but
that all of them will come to life as you believe and affirm God's
presence in you.

Recollect God in the year past—all the great work he did. Anticipate him in the year ahead. Keep his commands; be strong; take
possession of the land. Do that and you will be prepared a year
from now for the evening when you sit down and put up your feet
and someone comes into the room and says, "Anything interesting
happen this year?" You will have an answer: "My eyes have seen all
the great work that the Lord has done."

Review the past year and note the ways you saw God work in your
life and in your world. Tell someone else so you both can gain encouragement from God's work.

A Spiritual Skill That Can Renew Your Life

GOD said to me, "They're right; they've spoken the truth. I'll raise up for them a prophet like you from their kinsmen. I'll tell him what to say and he will pass on to them everything I command him. And anyone who won't listen to my words spoken by him, I will personally hold responsible."

—Deuteronomy 18:17–19

How do you shut out the noise long enough to hear the noel? How do you train yourself into that discipline that can tune out the cacophonous racket of the world so that you can hear the angel symphony singing God's glory in the highest? Your listening ear becomes the most responsible gift you can bring. You can give your attention, your mental alertness, your curiosity, and your intelligence. Listening is not only a function of biological acoustics; it is a spiritual skill of the soul.

There is something being said to you by the prophet who is like Moses, something said that is designed to rule your life, to lead you into a new way of existence, something that can evoke a response that has eternal dimensions to it. Don't be misled by the child in the manger. He really was a child, but he is of the family of Moses and he speaks. He says that you are loved by God, that you are accepted by God, that your life has an eternal meaning and destiny. Do I hear you say that you have heard all that before? No, that is a crashing, enlivening, beautiful new word. Once you hear that, you will never hear anything old again. Everything will be new. That is the kind of thing that keeps sounding new every time it is heard.

Separate yourself from all the noise and ask Jesus to tell you about yourself and about your tomorrow. Then listen carefully. Practice this spiritual skill of the soul.

DAY 18

God Ordains Strength and Courage

Haven't I commanded you? Strength! Courage!
Don't be timid; don't get discouraged. GOD, your
God, is with you every step you take.

—Joshua 1:9

The death of Moses was a crisis time. Israel never had, before or after, a leader like Moses. It was one of those impossible tasks of leadership, following a man whom you could never hope to equal. Making the leadership task even more difficult was the challenge before them: Canaan. It was a good land, flowing with milk and honey, but there were people already living in it who would not take kindly to the Jews coming in and waving the promise of God in front of their eyes. There was going to be a battle. And for the battle, there was going to have to be a leader. And Moses was dead.

Joshua was in the place where leadership often collapses: the great leader was dead, and the successor was clearly not of his stature. And the outside pressures were immediately intensified. The inward sense of worthiness and confidence was at a low ebb at the same time the outside pressure increased. The possibility of failure was clearly high. And that, no doubt, was why God repeated to Joshua, "Strength! Courage!" Three times God said this to Joshua. He was a man under orders. He was a man accompanied by his Lord. Regardless of his inner feelings, despite all threats from without, he was to be strong and of good courage. His life was an unfolding of his obedience to that command.

Joshua lacked confidence in his abilities right at the time he faced an impossible task. That's when God commanded him to be strong. To fail to be strong and of good courage would be disobedience. Think of ways God is commanding you to do the same.

Memorialize God's
Work in Your Life

He told the People of Israel, "In the days to come,
when your children ask their fathers, 'What are
these stones doing here?' tell your children this:
'Israel crossed over this Jordan on dry ground.'"

—Joshua 4:21–22

Joshua led the people through the Jordan. It was a miracle on
the same scale as the Red Sea crossing under Moses. The river
divided, and the people marched through safely. Then Joshua did
a very interesting thing. He had twelve men, one from each of the
tribes, take a stone out of the exposed riverbed and carry it to the
Canaan side. There they set the stones up as a memorial altar. And
then, with the people safely across and the stones set up, the river
resumed its course.

The people were ready to conquer the land. But lest the meaning of their future as the redeemed people of God be lost, they
built the twelve-stone altar. That altar was to be a witness to future
generations of God's action at the root of their lives. It was to stand

as a monument to his presence in time of need, an architectural witness to "how strong GOD's rescuing hand is" (verse 24). Joshua addressed the people: "In the days to come, when your children ask their fathers, 'What are these stones doing here?'" (verse 21). Answer: The existence of that altar, the architecture of that place of worship, contained a meaning that was to remain central to the people of Israel from that time down to our own.

Think of symbols of God's redemption that you hold on to—small artifacts, simple things that speak of his faithfulness to you. Show a few of these memorials to someone as you review God's faithfulness in the past and look forward to the days to come.

If You Know God, Miracles Aren't Mysterious

No more manna; the manna stopped. As soon as they started eating food grown in the land, there was no more manna for the People of Israel. That year they ate from the crops of Canaan.

—Joshua 5:12

iracle. It is badly identified when it is thought to mean that which we don't understand. That's the popular way the word is used, but it's not the Christian way. When something happens that we can't explain, we say that's a miracle. Under that set of definitions, most things that a magician does would be a miracle to me, and I know good and well they aren't. Miracle, through the biblical tradition, is not what we don't understand but what is done for us that we can't do ourselves. Miracle is functional. It's what God does for us or does for us through other people that we can't do ourselves.

It's possible you could understand it, but even if you did, that wouldn't make it stop being a miracle. The word does not mean that which is beyond our comprehension but rather that which is beyond our ability. So in that way I can, when I walk out in the morning and see the sun coming up over the horizon, say, "That's a miracle." And I would be biblically correct. Every morning is a miracle.

If God didn't excel at doing what we can't do for ourselves, he wouldn't be God. With that in mind, we see that his default approach to humanity is to work functional miracles. It's not a mystery—it's God.

Justice and Mercy
Go Together

GOD spoke to Joshua: "Tell the People of Israel:
Designate the asylum-cities, as I instructed you
through Moses, so that anyone who kills a person accidentally—that is, unintentionally—may
flee there as a safe place of asylum from the
avenger of blood."

—Joshua 20:1-3

Moses had given the initial instruction. It is described in both Numbers and Deuteronomy. The desert world at that time was regulated by the vendetta. If a man was killed, the slayer was hunted down by the relatives of the dead man and brought to swift account. It was a cruel, merciless justice. There were no courts, no trials, no arguments. One man was dead, so another must die to pay for it. But God's people were to show the way to something better. They were not to assume the legal presuppositions of the world in which they moved. They were to create something better, something more humane, something that took into account the complexity of the human situation and dealt with it with both justice and mercy.

So there was the command to designate six cities as "cities of refuge" (Numbers 35:6, RSV): Kedesh, Shechem, Hebron, Bezer, Ramoth, and Golan. At the city gates the guilty person would explain to the elders of the city the circumstances surrounding the killing. They would receive him and take responsibility for him and bring him to trial before the congregation of the people. They would decide whether it had been, in fact, an accidental killing or whether it had been deliberate. Cities of refuge guaranteed a fair hearing, a judicial trial, and protection until the final decision.

With God, it is not a matter of justice *or* mercy, but justice *and* mercy. In his nature, pure righteousness sees everything that is needed and works accordingly for the benefit of humanity.

Choose Because You're Chosen

As for me and my family, we'll worship GOD.

—Joshua 24:15

Joshua doesn't spend any time deriding the religious options that are before the people. He does not argue his case. He simply sorts out the possibilities and demands that the people make up their minds. I find that highly instructive. What Joshua does for the Hebrews, he does for you. Will you choose a religion of the past—of old stories, of nostalgia, of racial memories? Will you choose a religion because it is powerful, because it is associated with the winners, in the hope that you will acquire prestige, reputation, and influence? Will you choose a religion of good luck, a practical, down-to-earth kind of thing that will promise you success in your daily life? Or will you choose the God who has chosen you—the God who in Jesus Christ said that he loved you and wanted you to live as his child?

Am I looking for a religion that will fill in the vacant places in my life, shopping around for a religion that will benefit me? Or will

I respond to the most powerful and convincing word of love that has ever been spoken and simply say yes, in faith, to that word and live as Christ's disciple?

What has delivered you from forces that would destroy you? Religion or following Christ? The pursuit of power, success, and status—or the pursuit of God? Joshua told the people where he stood. Where do you stand?

God Knows Our Needs from Our Wants

If you decide that it's a bad thing to worship GOD, then choose a god you'd rather serve—and do it today. Choose one of the gods your ancestors worshiped from the country beyond The River, or one of the gods of the Amorites, on whose land you're now living. As for me and my family, we'll worship GOD.

—Joshua 24:15

*S*erve is one of the great clarifying words in Scripture. The Messiah is described in Isaiah as the servant of the Lord (see Isaiah 50:10). Paul described himself as a servant of Jesus Christ (see Philippians 1:1). We in the Christian community are told to be servants of one another in love (see Galatians 5:13). Most other religions look at this differently. They turn the idea of serve around: God is the servant of man. If we know the right gods and the right things to do, we can get them to do for us what we can't do for ourselves. Non-biblical religions are complex mechanisms for manipulating the gods for our own pleasure.

Most of us want a god who will serve us and get us what we want. We are never wholly successful in eliminating such impulses and fantasies. But when we look around us and see the people who always do get what they want, we don't see a very attractive picture. When children are reared under those conditions, we call them "spoiled." When adults get what they want, they turn out to be extraordinarily insensitive and curiously unhappy, for what we want is not what we need. A life saturated in consumer products and inundated with diversions seems only to breed restlessness and boredom.

A false god might promise to deliver everything you want. The one true God promises to always meet your needs. If you seek to gain everything you want, you'll be disappointed in him.

DAY 24

Obedience Means Adhering to God's Promises

> GOD faced him directly: "Go in this strength that is yours. Save Israel from Midian. Haven't I just sent you?"
>
> —Judges 6:14

So many times in the biblical narratives, we learn more of ourselves in reading them than we do of ancient history. The words of Gideon's question leap as readily to our lips: "If the LORD is with us, why then has all this befallen us?" (verse 13, RSV). God seems so far away when our lives are filled with death, suffering, boredom, jobs we don't like, people we don't understand, circumstances we can't change. We listen for the answer to Gideon's question in hopes we may hear an answer to our own. But as so often happens in the encounters between God and man in the Bible, there is no answer, at least not what we would ordinarily classify as an answer. Rather, there is a command: "Save Israel from Midian." Gideon's response is much like ours would be: "Look at me. My clan's the weakest in Manasseh and I'm the runt of the litter" (verse

15). Again comes an answer that is not quite an answer but rather a command plus a promise. There was to be no more introspection over past failures, no speculation on the ways of fate, no self-evaluation. The initiative was in God's hands, as it had been back in Egypt. Gideon had only to obey and adhere to the promise. He had only to serve, and God would bring the victory.

God is known for linking a promise to a command. It's as if he gives us instructions and, knowing how daunting this is for us, hurries to remind us of his presence, power, and help. Obeying God is not easy, but neither is it a solo pursuit.

A Subplot to the Story of Salvation

Once upon a time—it was back in the days when judges led Israel—there was a famine in the land. A man from Bethlehem in Judah left home to live in the country of Moab, he and his wife and his two sons. The man's name was Elimelech; his wife's name was Naomi; his sons were named Mahlon and Kilion—all Ephrathites from Bethlehem in Judah. They all went to the country of Moab and settled there.

—Ruth 1:1-2

I n the days when . . ." It's essentially "Once upon a time," the way all good stories begin. It is also the way Christians deal with the question "Does my life matter?" In a story every character is essential. Every person has significance. Only bad writers put in fluff and filler. God is not a bad writer. So we say "Once upon a time" and follow with our faith and our doubt, our obedience and our disobedience, our worship and our indifference. All of that and more is part of a story—a story that means something.

Not all stories are about heroes. Not all stories are epic

adventures. We do have heroic stories—those of Joseph and Moses and David and Paul. But there are also stories like that of Naomi and Ruth and Boaz. Here the action is very everyday. But all that everyday action—the immigration, the loyalty of Ruth to Naomi, the kindness of Boaz to Ruth, the attentiveness to the Law—all these details are part of a story that is a subplot in God's great salvation story. The story that means something—and also means everything.

The story of God's interventions in your life is a significant subplot to the bigger story of his bringing salvation to the world. Take some time to review the chapters of his story of salvation in your life.

A Biblical Complaint Against God

> The two of them traveled on together to Bethlehem.
>
> When they arrived in Bethlehem the whole town was soon buzzing: "Is this really our Naomi? And after all this time!"
>
> But she said, "Don't call me Naomi; call me Bitter. The Strong One has dealt me a bitter blow."
>
> —Ruth 1:19–20

Naomi got into the story by complaining. She experienced loss, complained bitterly about it, had her unhappiness taken seriously by the storyteller and formulated into a complaint against God. These verses are worded in such a way that she is presented as a plaintiff before God. This style of complaining put into legal form was also spoken by Jeremiah, who engaged in suit and countersuit between God and the people. He took up the people's complaints and pressed them into a legal suit against God; the accusation was that God had failed to be just and fair.

Even though it seems impious, even blasphemous, to talk this way to God, the plain fact is that it is thoroughly biblical. By listening to each other's complaints and formulating them against God, we help one another get into the story. We don't always have to be on God's side, defending him. There are times when our biblical position is at the plaintiff's side. By being taken seriously—not rejected, not toned down, not spiritualized—Naomi's complaint becomes part of the story. The emptiness of her life is woven into the story's plot and, in the process, becomes an occasion for demonstrating God's providence.

Do you hesitate to voice your complaints against God? Do you hear a nagging voice that says, *You can't possibly find fault with a perfect God*? Ruth's story is one of faith and obedience, yet Naomi's complaints loom large. How might this guide you in speaking to God with greater candor?

Life Is Righteous When It Benefits Others

Boaz then addressed the elders and all the people in the town square that day: "You are witnesses today that I have bought from Naomi everything that belonged to Elimelech and Kilion and Mahlon, including responsibility for Ruth the foreigner, the widow of Mahlon—I'll take her as my wife and keep the name of the deceased alive along with his inheritance. The memory and reputation of the deceased is not going to disappear out of this family or from his hometown. To all this you are witnesses this very day."

—Ruth 4:9-10

Some people, like Boaz, get into the story by taking up their responsibilities. They plunge into righteous living—living that models God's righteous relationships by going beyond the letter of the law and persistently and generously seeking ways to put their wealth and position to work on behalf of others. Because Boaz decides to act in this way, God's wings are experienced in the story through the wings of Boaz. Redemption is experienced in the story because Boaz works through the legal details of an old Mosaic law.

There are persons of substance who take their strength, their wealth, and their influence for granted and never use them in relation to others. We are in a position to collaborate with persons like this in such a way that they no longer see themselves as a center to which fame, possessions, and power naturally gravitate but as persons at the center of a circle of responsibilities. Boaz is named in the story as "one of our circle of covenant redeemers" (Ruth 2:20). He knew the function of the redeemer. The story gave him the opportunity to live up to the privilege of his responsibilities, and he seized it.

God includes us in his redeeming work, which extends to our involvement in helping others. For his people in the Old Testament, it was a matter of following the Law. Today it is a life of sharing the bounty we receive from him. Who needs to benefit from your riches?

Make Our Needs and Wants Known

Boaz married Ruth. She became his wife. Boaz slept with her. By GOD's gracious gift she conceived and had a son.

   The town women said to Naomi, "Blessed be GOD! He didn't leave you without family to carry on your life."

—Ruth 4:13-14

Being in God's story does not mean passively letting things happen to us. It doesn't mean dumb submission or blind obedience. Alien though she is (and her foreignness is repeatedly emphasized; six times in the RSV she is called "the Moabitess") and outside the defined covenant boundaries, Ruth gets into the story when she steps out of the roles in which she has been placed by others—the role of daughter-in-law, the role of Moabitess, the role of gleaner—and speaks her own lines: "Marry me!" The custom of the times held that placing a garment over a woman during these harvest rituals was a symbolic claim to marriage. In other words, Ruth says, "I want you to marry me." The consequence is that she enters into the center of the action and becomes an ancestress of the Messiah.

There are times when we help each other get into the story by encouraging one another to step out and speak our own lines—and not just parrot what we have been coached in by mother and father, spouse and teacher, pastor and evangelist. Story making is creative not only in its arranging of materials, not only in paying attention to the overlooked realities of the hidden ways of God, but also, at the right time, speaking up and asking for what we want.

God gave you a voice. And being human, you have wants and needs. None of us is self-sufficient; we aren't designed that way. Which needs or wants have you been reluctant to voice?

Finding Unity Under God's Kingship

> Samuel then addressed the people, "Take a good look at whom GOD has chosen: the best! No one like him in the whole country!"
>
> Then a great shout went up from the people: "Long live the king!"
>
> Samuel went on to instruct the people in the rules and regulations involved in a kingdom, wrote it all down in a book, and placed it before GOD. Then Samuel sent everyone home.
>
> —1 Samuel 10:24–25

Until the time of Samuel in the eleventh century BC, Israel functioned without a king. To put it another way, the Hebrews were nearly a thousand years old as a nation before they had their first king. Beginning with Abraham and through the age of the patriarchs, Israel was a nomadic tribe, moving from place to place. After that, four hundred years were spent in Egyptian slavery, and this, as much as anything else, transformed them into a nation. Moses led them out of slavery, and they were given a law at

Sinai and a land in Canaan. No government as such was instituted. When they entered Canaan, all the ingredients of national life were at hand: a law, a land, and a leader. The only unusual item was in that last piece—God was their leader.

From time to time, prophetic voices called judges were raised up to speak for God. But that was an irregular thing, and for the most part, the tribes took care of their own affairs internally. It was a crude government very strong on states' rights. And in the end was ineffective, a dark chapter in Israel's long and convoluted story.

Right before our eyes the Hebrew nation makes this mighty transition from a loose confederacy of tribes to the strong central monarchy. But the refusal to look ultimately to God as King is an indictment clear to anyone with eyes to see or ears to hear. Consider your political allegiances in light of Israel's lessons.

DAY 30

God Surpasses Earthly Power

When you saw Nahash, king of the Ammonites, preparing to attack you, you said to me, "No more of this. We want a king to lead us." And GOD was already your king!

So here's the king you wanted, the king you asked for. GOD has let you have your own way, given you a king.

—1 Samuel 12:12–13

If a Christian wants to live life as a unity where faith expresses itself in existence, if a Christian wants to avoid having life split into two parts—the part of God and the part of the world, the part of religion and the part of politics—then it is necessary to reflect with courage on the following question: "How does Christ help me live as a political person?" In searching the Scriptures, here are two things worth reflection.

First, the biblical individual was always intensely involved in the political world—participated in it, prayed in it, was always in relationship with it. Politics was never a matter of indifference.

Second, it didn't seem to make too much difference who was in political power. Politics was never the ultimate power for biblical individuals. For them, political regimes were like houses: they were important, you spent a lot of time and attention on them, but the model wasn't terribly important really. Any style was livable, and even if you didn't have one at all, there were things that could make life meaningful and rich.

A biblical snapshot would be intense involvement in political affairs with a conviction that the ultimate power is in God, not political systems.

A biblical view of citizenship takes into account two worlds: earthly life in concert with others and God's reign over everything. God's reign helps us keep earthly matters such as political systems, loyalties, and policies in perspective. How does God's kingship guide your political commitments?

Allegiance to God Shows in Your Life

GOD spoke to Samuel: "I'm sorry I ever made Saul king. He's turned his back on me. He refuses to do what I tell him."

—1 Samuel 15:10–11

D o you remember the parable our Lord told about the man who desired to build a tower? He had great ambitions and high hopes. But he didn't first sit down and count the cost. He just started building. He probably talked a lot about it, put out some publicity, made a splash. But putting in the foundation was as far as he got. People walked by and said, "This man began to build and was not able to finish."

Do you remember that other time when it became popular to follow Jesus and several came to him and announced their discipleship but each one put in a condition? The last one said, "I'm ready to follow you, Master, but first excuse me while I get things straightened out at home" (Luke 9:61). Jesus said to him, "No procrastination. No backward looks. You can't put God's kingdom off till tomorrow. Seize the day" (verse 62).

King Saul fits this pattern. There is a vigorous beginning. There is a declared conviction. There seems to be a great future. But internally there is a fatal flaw that shows up sooner than anyone would have thought possible. We never see the finished building. We never see the consummated discipleship. For all his physical prowess and his popular attraction, Saul was basically defective in understanding the kingship of God. Because he was the king, he assumed that everything, even God, was at his disposal. But God will not be used.

The working out of God's will on earth includes us, but it doesn't rely on us. From a human perspective, Saul was perfect king material. But by God's measure, Saul was a supreme mistake. How do you guard against the tendency to rely on human standards?

Be Careful to Avoid the Seeds of Failure

Samuel said,
> Do you think all GOD wants are
>   sacrifices—
>   empty rituals just for show?
> He wants you to listen to him!
> Plain listening is the thing,
>   not staging a lavish religious
>   production.
> Not doing what GOD tells you
>   is far worse than fooling around in the
>   occult.
> Getting self-important around GOD
>   is far worse than making deals with
>   your dead ancestors.
> Because you said No to GOD's command,
>   he says No to your kingship.

—1 Samuel 15:22–23

This is virtually the end of King Saul. His very auspicious reign begun with glamor and launched with success quickly disintegrates. The rest of his reign is actually the story of the rise of David. Saul is only the background figure for the one who will displace him. The last we see of him is as a disguised, mentally deranged old man, going by night to the witch of Endor to inquire through her mediumship of his fate. The next day he and his sons die in battle.

Note the series of contrasts in the life of Saul. He begins in obedience, going out at his father's command looking for donkeys. He ends in disobedience, making the sacrifice at Gilgal and looting the livestock of the Amalekites. He begins with a great sense of mercy and compassion. He ends in bitter vengeance, trying to murder David. He begins with the spirit of God descending upon him. He ends with the absence of God's spirit. He begins near Superman and ends a pitiful suicide. Outwardly all was success, but inwardly the seeds of failure bloomed.

What should have been an inspiring history of Saul's reign is instead a tragic account of decline and self-destruction. The Bible tells Saul's story to show us how to avoid the seeds of failure by obeying God. In what ways have you seen people invest in their own failure?

A Character That Counts

> David sang this lament over Saul and his son
> Jonathan, and gave orders that everyone in
> Judah learn it by heart. Yes, it's even inscribed
> in The Book of Jashar.
> > Oh, oh, Gazelles of Israel, struck down on
> > your hills,
> > the mighty warriors—fallen, fallen!
>
> —2 Samuel 1:17–19

Death is a favorite theme with novelists. In the intense interplay of feelings, character is revealed. The actual character of men and women emerges in confrontation with the ultimate issues. Forces that have been dormant or hidden beneath the routine surfaces of life suddenly are exposed, and not infrequently the exposure is of ugliness and malice.

David, who might well have responded with glee to the Amalekite's self-serving lie, didn't tolerate it for a minute. He saw through its fabrication and its slander. He punished the man on the spot and had him executed. David was heir apparent to the throne. His years of hiding in the wilderness were over. His life in a cave would now be changed to a palace hall.

But none of that played a part in David's response to the tragedy. His response was all lament. He participated in the tragedy as one who had loved deeply and selflessly. His own troubles with Saul were minor compared with his loyalty to Saul and his love for Jonathan.

The character that had been building through those hard years in the wilderness was revealed to be one marked by compassion and sensitivity, not nurtured on revenge and hate. The song that he sang is one of the saddest and most powerful laments in the literature of the world.

Worship Sanctifies
Time and Space

That night, the word of GOD came to Nathan saying, "Go and tell my servant David: This is GOD's word on the matter: You're going to build a 'house' for me to live in? Why, I haven't lived in a 'house' from the time I brought the children of Israel up from Egypt till now. All that time I've moved about with nothing but a tent. And in all my travels with Israel, did I ever say to any of the leaders I commanded to shepherd Israel, 'Why haven't you built me a house of cedar?'"

—2 Samuel 7:4–7

For a trapeze artist, success or failure—sometimes life or death—is determined by fractions of inches, split seconds of time. In ordinary life, a few inches more or less make no difference. Five seconds or five minutes early or late cause little difficulty. But in the precision world of the trapeze, both time and space have critical importance.

Christian worship is the sanctification of time and space. That which we look at, live in, and treat casually in ordinary life is concentrated into the hour of Christian worship so that we see its ultimate and eternal meaning. Worship gives a heightened significance to the time and space of the ordinary world. No one could, nor would want to, live in the intense world of worship all the time. But worship does give a sharpness to everything the Christian does. The Christian leaving the hour of worship knows that love, hope, faith, praise, blessing, and grace provide the fractional differences, in minute quantities, that make the eternal difference in life. The Christian at worship is like an aerial gymnast on a trapeze. She experiences the meaning of time and space. When she moves back into her ordinary universe, there will be sharpness and accuracy to her feelings and her actions that were not there before.

Meeting God in worship shifts the focus from self to the holy. Worship gives "a sharpness" to the rest of a Christian's life. Weigh the meaning of those words as you consider the gifts that come from worship.

False Substitutes
for God's Rule

> Absalom sent undercover agents to all the tribes
> of Israel with the message, "When you hear the
> blast of the ram's horn trumpet, that's your sig-
> nal: Shout, 'Absalom is king in Hebron!'"

> —2 Samuel 15:10

The narrative has made clear that what is being talked about here is the rule of God. He anointed David as king to represent his rule over his people. There has been no attempt to portray David as a perfect man or a perfect ruler. In fact, there is great candidness and openness about his failings and sins. But all the same, it is the rule of God that is being represented. This is the same rule that is given perfect and complete expression in the event of Jesus Christ.

The whole Absalom incident is told in the context of God's rule. And it is this that is underneath the story theologically. There is much other interest that gathers around the story: the rather pathetic picture of David's inept fatherhood, the revolutionary insurrection of Absalom, the politics of violence in the burning of the barley field, and the style of political life engendered by Absalom. All that catches our attention, but at the bottom of it all, there is the decision that is being made to accept the rule of God or rebel against it.

Absalom represents the highly attractive, exceedingly plausible alternative to accepting God's rule. God rules us, but there are seductive alternatives, such as having the entire nation of Israel proclaim, "Absalom is king in Hebron!" Ponder two such seductions in your life right now—seductions that compete with God's rule.

Love Involves a Commitment to Others

The king ordered Joab and Abishai and Ittai, "Deal gently for my sake with the young man Absalom." The whole army heard what the king commanded the three captains regarding Absalom.

—2 Samuel 18:5

The revealing anecdote that proves David's decision to love Absalom is in a conversation David had with his generals the day he sent them out to battle. David had left family, home, rule, and throne in Jerusalem, along with temple, priests, and the ark of the covenant. The years of struggle to put the kingdom together on a sound administrative and military basis were smashed. Now, with his mercenary troops and his generals, he prepared for battle with the rebels. The strategy was agreed on, and then there was a last word with the three generals. David said, "Deal gently for my sake with the young man Absalom." The counsel rejected revenge and affirmed love. But for Joab, there was something more important than obeying the king's command: there was the demand that justice be served.

I must tell you, however, that David's way is best. However tragic, however sad, however painful, it is nevertheless authentically human and full of love. And it is the gospel. It is the same kind of humanity that Jesus fulfilled and displayed when he stood over Jerusalem and wept. David began something that Jesus completed and we must share: a commitment to others defined by love. And yes, this love exposes us to the pain of rejection and the grief of loss. This love is not easy. But to live another way is to live less than human.

King David's son Absalom set out to kill his father. In the midst of this, David did all he could to ensure his son's safety. God's love is persistent in his commitment to us, his rebellious people. Recall a time when you ran and God refused to let you go.

Humans Are Intensely Emotional

The king was stunned. Heartbroken, he went up to the room over the gate and wept. As he wept he cried out,

O my son Absalom, my dear, dear son Absalom!

Why not me rather than you, my death and not yours,

O Absalom, my dear, dear son!

—2 Samuel 18:33

To know that David is capable of such grief is to know something essential about him. Superficial, shallow people cannot grieve like this. David was a man with his emotions developed. He could be affected by tragedy and moved by disaster. David was not the wisest man in Hebrew history, not the saintliest or the best. But there is massed evidence to show that he was authentically, completely human. We don't get such a quantity of convincingly personal material about any other figure in Scripture, except for our Lord.

We need to associate with such a man and assimilate the material of his humanity. Our culture, for suppressed reasons, avoids intense feelings. We stay out of meetings, confrontations, reconciliations, and relationships that will exact any kind of emotional commitment. We dabble. And our world becomes flat and humorless. We try to get feeling from plastic and metal. But our emotional lives are so far atrophied that they won't be rehabilitated, so we compulsively travel and buy and talk.

Sadness, grief, lament—the occasions when humanity is most aware of its transience and its glory—are shunned. We become less than the full persons we are created to be.

David has been referred to as the greatest king of the united Israel. We think often of his greatness but far less about his egregious sins and common human weakness. Here we see his humanity. Jesus came, in part, to restore us to full humanity. This bears greater consideration.

King David's
Words to Live By

GOD, your light floods my path,
   GOD drives out the darkness.
I smash the bands of marauders,
   I vault the high fences.
What a God! His road
   stretches straight and smooth.
Every GOD-direction is road-tested.
   Everyone who runs toward him
Makes it.

—2 Samuel 22:29-31

I n genius fashion, David combined excellence in diplomacy, war, politics, government administration, and poetry. He would be a leading candidate for what Western history has called a Renaissance Man. Yet the church does not remember him for such things. He could have lost all the battles, failed in his foreign relations, even left his own government disorganized and we would still hold him just as high in our catalog of heroes. But why?

That for which the church remembers David is expressed in the brief compass of two sentences in a poem near the conclusion of the narration of his life. This poem was felt important enough to be put in twice: first in David's life story and also in the Psalms (see Psalm 18:28–30). The poem celebrates David's experience with God across a lifetime. He sings of the divine strength that took him as a fatigued and demoralized fugitive and transformed him into an empowered king. He exclaims,

> What a God! His road
>   stretches straight and smooth.
> Every GOD-direction is road-tested.
>   Everyone who runs toward him
> Makes it.

This has long stuck in my mind as being purely Davidic. It is the essence of his life to be saying something like this, and it would be hard to imagine anyone else saying it.

What is it about God and his work that can bring a common shepherd boy, later a hunted man even though he had been named the next king of Israel, to proclaim, "I smash the bands of marauders"? It is because "everyone who runs toward him makes it."

The Tragedy of Rejecting God's Wisdom

God gave Solomon wisdom—the deepest of understanding and the largest of hearts. There was nothing beyond him, nothing he couldn't handle. Solomon's wisdom outclassed the vaunted wisdom of wise men of the East, outshone the famous wisdom of Egypt.

—1 Kings 4:29-30

B ut with all his wealth and wisdom, Solomon failed to act wisely. His folly is revealed chiefly in his many wives. The record says, "King Solomon was obsessed with women" (1 Kings 11:1). This is flat defiance of the command of God not to marry into foreign lands. At that time these foreign nations were a deadly threat to the purity of Israel's religion. The narrative says that Solomon had "seven hundred royal wives and three hundred concubines. . . . As Solomon grew older, his wives beguiled him with their alien gods and he became unfaithful—he didn't stay true to his GOD as his father David had done" (verses 3–4).

After all the wise and practical proverbs he formulated about women and wives, he chose to ignore them in his own life. The result was a proliferation of pagan religion throughout the kingdom. In order to keep his homesick wives happy, he built them temples to their own gods. Unfortunately, the gods were base, cruel, sadistic, and immoral. Cult prostitution was part of some rituals, and child sacrifice was involved in others. The historian's summary of Solomon's foolishness was "Solomon took up with Ashtoreth, the whore goddess of the Sidonians, and Molech, the horrible god of the Ammonites. Solomon openly defied GOD; he did not follow in his father David's footsteps" (verses 5–6).

If the wisest man on earth was not immune to the folly of turning his back on God's wisdom, what hope is there for us if we do the same? The command here that Solomon disregarded was meant for his well-being, not to limit his freedom. Look for God's promise to you in every one of his commands.

Faith and Experience Dispel Doubt

Can it be that God will actually move into our neighborhood? Why, the cosmos itself isn't large enough to give you breathing room, let alone this Temple I've built. Even so, I'm bold to ask: Pay attention to these my prayers, both intercessory and personal, O GOD, my God. Listen to my prayers, energetic and devout, that I'm setting before you right now. Keep your eyes open to this Temple night and day, this place of which you said, "My Name will be honored there," and listen to the prayers that I pray at this place.

—1 Kings 8:27–29

As Solomon stands before the new temple with the people gathered around, he is suddenly struck with the absurdity of it all. He has spent a great deal of money and time to create a structure of worship, a holy place to which the people of Israel can come and worship God. And now when it is all finished, he asks the question we all do at one time or another: "Can it be that God will actually move into our neighborhood?" Solomon is assaulted by this reasoned skepticism and doubt, but he prays anyway. He prays that God will hear the people when they come to this house and offer their prayers, that God will be attentive to their needs night and day, and that when he hears them he will forgive.

The doubts have been repeated with variations from Solomon down to us. But we, like Solomon, have gone ahead and prayed anyway. The common-sense objection to God dwelling on earth in a house of prayer, to God meeting man in a place of worship, has not been able to survive the evidence of experience and faith. After all, common sense is one of the least reliable tests of reality. The cynical question "Can it be?" is answered by a deeper reason, a wider experience, and a realistic faith that says, "Yes, indeed!"

Can it be that God will actually move into our neighborhood? If you know God, you also know that you have encountered him in a multitude of ways—all of them on earth. Share some of those experiences with a trusted friend.

Prayer Lessons from History's Wisest Person

Keep your eyes open to this Temple night and day, this place of which you said, "My Name will be honored there," and listen to the prayers that I pray at this place.

Listen from your home in heaven and when you hear, forgive.

—1 Kings 8:29–30

In Solomon's prayer, we can see three areas in which the visible is a conduit for the invisible, and they are areas that we are still involved in today. The first has to do with history. Solomon brings into play the memory of the great encounters with God in the past. A poor memory is a threat to our prayers. The man who prays and forgets all the varied actions of God is apt to pray with small faith and for tiny ends.

The second has to do with forgiveness. Note that what Solomon prays for specifically is that God will forgive. Self-deception and selfishness are threats to our prayers as well. All too often our prayers are ways in which we can get God working on our side. But the visible church is a check against that. Forgiveness is the turning point in prayer, the transition from seeking our own way from God to yielding our lives to him so that he may perform his will in it.

The third area is mentioned by Solomon in the word *foreigner,* which can also be translated "stranger." Our prayers are strangled when they become too narrow. When our interest is exclusively on ourselves, our families, and small circles of acquaintances, we lose all sensitivity to the vast church of Christ and the world Christ is seeking to bring into fellowship with him. The visible church is a proof against that, bringing people together under one roof whom you would ordinarily not associate with.

Solomon in ancient times brought us three lessons in prayer, summarized in three words: history (God's work in the past), forgiveness (a turning point from self to God's will), and others (or strangers, foreigners). Look at the list of three and pray to God in light of the word that speaks most personally to you.

Tarnishing God's Glory

> In the fifth year of King Rehoboam's rule, Shishak king of Egypt made war against Jerusalem. He plundered The Temple of GOD and the royal palace of their treasures, cleaned them out—even the gold shields that Solomon had made. King Rehoboam replaced them with bronze shields and outfitted the royal palace guards with them.
>
> —1 Kings 14:25-27

The Bible is more interested in telling us about the inside than the outside. Because of that there is a revealing detail in the account of the Egyptian invasion. Solomon's shields of gold were ceremonial devices, used in the public worship of God. This probably had its origin in the time of David. He made gold shields to display in visible form the brilliant glory of God. But in Solomon's reign, the qualities that had made the gold shields meaningful slowly deteriorated. Loyalty to God, justice among the people, a vigilant protection of the freedom of the nation—these were all dissipated in Solomon's reign. From the outside the dissipation was not noticeable. The gold shields were still there. But under Rehoboam, the outward forms collapsed.

At least Rehoboam realized that it didn't look good to be deprived of shields. So he made more, with one small difference: this time they were made of bronze, the cheapest metal of the day. Those bronze shields sum up Rehoboam's reign. David experienced the splendor and glory of God. Solomon heard about such things and ensured the symbol stayed intact. But to Rehoboam, the splendor and glory were such distant memories that he was unaware how inadequate having bronze shields came across. The shields symbolized a cheapness of religion and a dullness of ritual that did not spring from immediate experience with the glory of God.

God knows everything revealed by our souls. Even in calling attention to God's glory in the symbolism of gold shields, Solomon had been true to him. But his son King Rehoboam didn't follow suit. Solomon's father, David, understood what we often overlook: God knows us better than we know ourselves (see Psalm 139).

A Very Human Messenger of God

She said to her mistress, "Oh, if only my master could meet the prophet of Samaria, he would be healed of his skin disease."

—2 Kings 5:3

One of the members of Naaman's household was a young girl who had been captured on one of his military raids into Israel. She had been made a slave in his house. She, of course, knew of his leprosy. She also became alert to the growing desperation in the man. This girl stands as a model of what it means to be God's witness. She is a link between Naaman's need and God's action. She is God's messenger.

She was a young slave in a foreign land. We would not be surprised to find such a person to be full of hatred, resentment, spite, and anger. But she did not do the expected. She shared her faith and hope with Naaman. She told him about God. It is not normal, and it is not expected, but God has such witnesses to his grace everywhere. The young girl was probably far from perfect.

She would have bad nights when she cried herself to sleep, lonely for her family in Israel.

But something else was dominant and overcame her inadequacies. She knew she was loved by God. And she knew he was in charge of the universe and of her life—she knew she could trust him to rule her. She was a messenger, from the Savior to the sinner. Scripture is full of such messengers, as is the church. I aspire to be among them.

We think of angelic beings as God's messengers, and they are. But so are we. Naaman was an enemy to the slave girl, who was a captive who might be expected to hate her abductor. Yet she shared God with her captor. Do you need to be a messenger of God to someone who has betrayed you?

What Gets in the Way of God's Work?

Naaman with his horses and chariots arrived in style and stopped at Elisha's door.

Elisha sent out a servant to meet him with this message: "Go to the River Jordan and immerse yourself seven times. Your skin will be healed and you'll be as good as new."

—2 Kings 5:9–10

The Jordan was a slow-moving, sluggish, murky river flowing indolently between muddy banks. Naaman had come from a mountain country where rivers sped rapidly and cleanly from cool mountain heights. The rivers in Syria were refreshing and clean; Jordan was a dirty creek, in contrast. Naaman was incensed and left in an understandable huff. As he left, he said, "I thought he'd personally come out and meet me" (verse 11).

How many times do we do that? We recognize our need, so we go to a church or a friend or a pastor for help. But then what is offered is so beneath our dignity or diverges so wildly from our expectations that we angrily go away. We are disappointed. We

wanted some excitement, some drama, some action, some original-
ity. We wanted some sensationalism. And what did we get? The
same old thing, the old virtues, the grace of God, and the love of
Christ.

But what do we have to lose, really? Maybe a little pride. And
what do we have to gain? Possibly everything. The real question is,
Do we want to be healed?

Do you find yourself in prayer, explaining to God how he should
go about helping someone? Have you ever missed something he did
because it didn't happen the way you had expected? Can you trust
God to act as he sees fit?

Religion Versus Knowing God

King Ahaz went to meet Tiglath-Pileser king of Assyria in Damascus. The altar in Damascus made a great impression on him. He sent back to Uriah the priest a drawing and set of blueprints of the altar. Uriah the priest built the altar to the specifications that King Ahaz had sent from Damascus. By the time the king returned from Damascus, Uriah had completed the altar.

—2 Kings 16:10-11

If Assyria was the strongest, most respected, most extensive world power, the Assyrian altar must have been the strongest, most respected, most extensive religious symbol. So Ahaz had his servants copy the dimensions of the altar and take them back to Jerusalem with instructions to make a replica. But the Assyrian altar did not represent atheism. Nor did it represent a repudiation of Israel's faith, at least not in an overt, public way. The Assyrian altar represented an increase in religious activity, a compulsive desire to have the best religion, the most powerful faith, to be up on the latest developments in theology and liturgical practice.

No doubt Ahaz was a very sincere, very honest, and very religious person loyal to the traditions of Moses and David and Solomon. The sin that he became involved in was a religious sin, and it proceeded from religious motives: to be secure, to be at the center of God's attention, to have a workable faith. If you are committed to a religious life, you will always be prey to the Assyrian altar of Ahaz. When failure or danger comes, that latest fad or the thing that seems to be working best will have a great attraction to you—spiritualism, the occult, astrology, a new sect, a new leader, a new book. The gospel is the dissolving of religion. God speaks in the form of the person, Jesus, and establishes not a religion but a relationship.

Have you wondered why Jesus didn't come to earth to establish Christianity, why he didn't invite people to become Christians? Instead, he called people to follow him. Take time to consider the difference.

How Sin Distorts the Fight Against Evil

Go and pray to GOD for me and for this people—
for all Judah! Find out what we must do in response to what is written in this book that has
just been found! GOD's anger must be burning furiously against us—our ancestors haven't
obeyed a thing written in this book, followed
none of the instructions directed to us.

—2 Kings 22:13

A typical reaction to discovering there is widespread evil in
the world is to want to get out your broom and sweep
the place clean. Righteous indignation blazes in the heart. Adrena-
line flows into the bloodstream. Something has to be done. But
the dangers that stem from the action need to be spelled out. The
most perilous action of the human being is the reforming action.
There are no areas where it is easier to fall into a kind of devastating
sin than here. The sins that derive from this are spiritual. One is
arrogance/hate/self-righteous pride. Another is corrosive anger. A
third is apathy.

So the question before us is, How do we do something in the face of the evil in the world while at the same time avoiding these sins? A good first step is don't conceal, don't avoid.

Concealment works two ways: you can conceal the evil, or you can conceal the Word of God. But in either case what happens is that the two are kept apart from a recognized relationship. Once you put them both on the table together, they are connected in death and resurrection. And the nature of this world as the gospel sees it is not as a battle between good and evil but a movement of death and resurrection.

What's your tendency—to conceal or avoid the evil, or to conceal (possibly mute) God's Word? Do you have any idea as to the origin of that tendency? What would it look like to refuse to conceal either?

God Speaks in a Whirlwind of Loss

I admit I once lived by rumors of you;
  now I have it all firsthand—from my own
  eyes and ears!

—Job 42:5

The book of Job is the story of the penetration of God's grace through layers of doubt, suffering, defiance, indifference, and, most of all, trite and hackneyed religion, to the inner heart of man. It is a story of a man surrounded by the evidence for God's existence, and much religious talk of God's power and purpose, who suddenly becomes confronted by God himself and is made whole in the confrontation.

The heart of the book consists of a dialogue between Job and three friends, to which is added the speech of a fourth friend, and concludes with the voice of God "out of the whirlwind" (Job 38:1, RSV). Job has lost all that he counted valuable: vast wealth, a prosperous family, and his health. Disaster has wiped out his livestock, his children have been killed, and he has been afflicted by a painful case of boils.

When his friends try to advise him, they only make matters worse. Job calls them "miserable comforters" (16:2) and "pompous quacks" (13:4). But even in the face of such total rejection, Job harbors an invincible hope: "Still, I know that God lives—the One who gives me back my life—and eventually he'll take his stand on earth. And I'll see him—even though I get skinned alive!—see God myself, with my very own eyes. Oh, how I long for that day!" (19:25–27).

Has God ever taken away people, relationships, and things you treasure? Are you able to view the loss of what you valued so highly as his work to clear away distractions so you can see him more clearly?

Condemning Others to Justify Ourselves

A spirit glided right in front of me—
the hair on my head stood on end.

—Job 4:15

Eliphaz is Job's first friend. He begins his speech with a ghost story. Out of this comes a message, supposedly with the authority of the supernatural behind it. Eliphaz finds the source of Job's trouble in sin. His reasoning goes like this: sin causes suffering, Job is suffering, so therefore Job is a sinner. It matters not that Job protests his innocence. This just means that Job is not only a sinner but a liar on top of that.

Eliphaz says, "Mortals are born and bred for trouble, as certainly as sparks fly upward" (Job 5:7). He then proceeds to discover in Job the sin that is at the root of all his trouble. He accuses him of a variety of misdeeds and seeks to bring Job to a point of confession and abasement. Eliphaz is a dogmatist who uses other men's misfortunes as illustrations of the truth of his dogma. Job is a convenient illustration of a major tenet in his theology.

Has a friend ever told you that if your faith had been stronger, if you hadn't strayed outside God's will, or if you had prayed more, you would not have had to endure some major setback? How did you respond?

Our Significance in Light of God

How can you keep on talking like this?
You're talking nonsense, and noisy
nonsense at that.

—Job 8:2

Bildad, the second friend, tells Job that whatever else takes place, he must remember that God is the most important part of existence and Job must be careful not to blaspheme or deny him. The reason we cannot understand God is that he is so great and we are so insignificant. How can we hope to understand such a vast purpose and a mighty mind that must operate in the counsels of God?

But in magnifying God, Bildad minimizes man and suggests that because man is so insignificant, little better than a maggot or worm, he really cannot expect any better treatment. God must have a very busy schedule, and man is a tiny part of the historical scene, so Job ought to forget about understanding his own part in it. It is enough to know that God has a vast purpose running through the universe.

Bildad is a traditionalist who can spin beautiful and convincing philosophical ideas but who has no ability to apply them in a human way to the personal details of life. He is very good at talking about God and history and the future, but he can never remember his wedding anniversary.

Here is a truth that Bildad overlooks: "Why do you bother with us? Why take a second look our way?" (Psalm 8:4). The question leads to one conclusion: God created humanity and would never lose sight of us. Never.

The Danger of Poorly Aimed Zeal

Your world will be washed in sunshine,
every shadow dispersed by dayspring.

—Job 11:17

Zophar, the third friend, is a pious moralist. It's easy to determine this. He advises Job:

Still, if you set your heart on God
  and reach out to him,
If you scrub your hands of sin
  and refuse to entertain evil in your home,
You'll be able to face the world unashamed
  and keep a firm grip on life, guiltless and fearless.
You'll forget your troubles;
  they'll be like old, faded photographs.
Your world will be washed in sunshine,
  every shadow dispersed by dayspring. (11:13–17)

Zophar is not only straight, but he is also narrow. He is the zealot for the justice of God. His mission is to hustle people on the road to good works. Job must do good deeds, and then his problem will be solved. Zophar has the universe well ordered in his mind, and Job is a disorderly spot in it. He must be put in order much as a meticulous housewife straightens a crooked picture or removes a smudge.

Zophar is impatient with Job. He insults him and accuses him. Zophar is on God's side and wants to clean the world up. He never really hears Job's story or becomes sensitive to his plight. He is eager to jump in and sort out the case and apply his puritan zeal to the reformation of Job's life.

Is life generally orderly or mostly chaotic? When God broke through the status quo by living among us, did people calmly note his presence, or did a storm of change break out? God's work upsets things. One more time: God's work upsets things.

Can Enthusiasm Substitute for Wisdom?

I'm a young man,
   and you are all old and experienced.
That's why I kept quiet
   and held back from joining the
      discussion.

—Job 32:6

Elihu is the fourth speaker. He has not spoken before. The reason is that he is very young. But now he cannot be quiet any longer—he is ready to burst with his advice. He says that he has listened carefully to the preceding advice and to Job's defense and found both very weak. Conclusion: "Getting old doesn't guarantee good sense" (verse 9). Always when youth assays to play its part, it begins with impatience and often rightly so. Youth was not born to a mold, and much of what has been passed down to it is warped and twisted by the past.

But is it really necessary to demolish everything and begin afresh? To, as they say, throw the baby out with the bathwater? I overheard a young college student say, "I have heard a good many preachers, and I have read a good many religious books. Now I have made up my mind that all of it has to go. I must begin for myself and begin from scratch." That rarely works in life, much less in a religion.

Still, untrammeled by the traditions that bound his elders, Elihu speaks truth somewhat better than Job's other friends. But when all is said and done, he has said nothing new.

It is rarely necessary to clear the board and start over. The baby should only on occasion be thrown out with the bathwater. Recall a time when you threw both out. What were the results—in the moment and also in retrospect?

Praying, Again, in Desperation

You, GOD, shield me on all sides;
You ground my feet, you lift my head high;
With all my might I shout up to GOD,
His answers thunder from the holy
    mountain.

—Psalm 3:3–4

The third psalm is attributed to David "when he fled from Absalom his son" (RSV). Psalm titles are not always reliable, and each of them was affixed later than the psalm itself. But this one is imaginative at heart. The psalmist is in a position of trouble. He is overwhelmed by hostile forces, the victim of a massive assault. He is alone against many, in an exposed position.

David is in the deepest kind of trouble. He prays from a position of sheer desperation. Circumstance presents a unified front against him in the rebellion of Absalom, and faith in God's help is shattered by the act and counsel of Ahithophel. Military realities and political wisdom proclaim David a doomed man. The combination of Absalom and Ahithophel pushes David to the wall.

Desperate as David's circumstances are, and as short on alternatives as he is, we would be wrong in assuming that prayer here is the evidence of "foxhole religion." When he writes, "I shout up to GOD" (Psalm 3:4), the Hebrew tense (imperfect) means that this is a habitual act in his life. In other words, he is not praying for the first time or just in emergencies. His praying is effective now because he is already skilled at it.

Recall a time when all the signs pointed against you, when you came close to giving up, but you asked God to intervene and he came through. He restored hope and restored you in the process. Tell someone about his work of restoration.

Moods Are Fickle, but God Is Faithful

I bless GOD every chance I get;
my lungs expand with his praise.
I live and breathe GOD;
if things aren't going well, hear this
and be happy:
Join me in spreading the news;
together let's get the word out.

—Psalm 34:1-3

One of the common mistakes we Christians make is to try to draw some transcendent meaning out of the good days and bad days, to suppose that we are better Christians on good days and worse Christians on bad days. Moods lie, and emotions deceive. A persistent task of preaching is to keep a congregation in touch with a way of life that is rooted in a faithful God, not in fickle moods. Psalm 34 is at hand to be used for such a purpose. It describes a life that has all the contrasts in it—up and down, black and white, sunshine and drizzle—but it doesn't separate them into good days and bad days. It combines them all in a life of blessing.

The psalm's first sentence, in the RSV, seems impossible and invites contradiction. But if you look more closely at the text, you will find that it does not say, "I will be happy at all times," but "I will bless the LORD at all times." Another way to translate that, a way that catches the idiom of everyday life better, is "I will bless GOD every chance I get; my lungs expand with his praise." This is not a person whose moods are steadily ebullient but a person who has simply decided to speak a word of blessing every chance he gets, determined to be in readiness to give a praising word.

Are you lying if you thank God when you don't feel thankful? Is it hypocritical to praise him when you're on the verge of losing your faith? Speak the truth no matter how you're feeling. It will remain long after your feelings change.

Longing for God's Freshness

A white-tailed deer drinks
from the creek;
I want to drink God,
deep draughts of God.

—Psalm 42:1

A deer thirsty for water is the metaphor. What water is to the deer, God is to me. I simply must have God. And it must be the living God. Nothing stale or stagnant. The deer runs past all the mud puddles and swamps and marshes to clear, flowing streams. I don't want my God out of a bottle. I don't want what is left over from God after last week's thundershower. I want him fresh, flowing, living. What I learned in Sunday school in the third grade will not satisfy me. What I read in the Bible last week will not satisfy me. What someone told me this morning on television or radio will not quench my thirst. I want to get to the water myself. I must have God.

Every natural appetite is a reminder of this thirst for God. Every thirst, every hunger, every longing for satisfaction—it is a metaphor for the fundamental desire in our lives for God.

The writer of Lamentations says that God's mercies are created new every morning (see 3:23). God did not go on hiatus last week or last year. He is present at the start of every day and when you go to sleep at night. Don't rely on a dim memory of God; seek him in every moment.

God's Actions Prompt Worship

Loud cheers as God climbs the mountain,
a ram's horn blast at the summit.
Sing songs to God, sing out!
Sing to our King, sing praise!
He's Lord over earth,
so sing your best songs to God.

—Psalm 47:5–7

As this psalm was sung in ancient Israel, they were gathered in congregational worship much as we are today. Three things are prominent in their singing and praying that are instructive for us. One, the psalm pivots on the action of God. His triumphant movement initiates the congregation's worship. Take that away and you wouldn't have anything. Two, note that the character of God's action determines the character of the worship. His action is triumphant and kingly; he is over all the earth and rules all men. So the worship reflects this by shouts of joy and songs of praise. We say things and sing things in worship that are appropriate to God's action. Three, the psalm calls for total congregational participation.

"All peoples" (verse 1, RSV) are involved. It is impossible to imagine this psalm being sung by an isolated priest or singer in the middle of a crowd of Hebrews. No, everyone is involved in the singing and praying of this psalm. The action of God is central to the whole nation, and the whole nation is involved in a response while gathering in celebration and worship.

God's work prompts our worship. His involvement with humanity is not to be disregarded or forgotten. Of course, he would remain the same with or without our worship, but we would not. Join with other believers in the worship of him.

Seek God,
Not His Creation

Drench the plowed fields,
   soak the dirt clods
With rainfall as harrow and rake
   bring her to blossom and fruit.
Snow-crown the peaks with splendor,
   scatter rose petals down your paths,
All through the wild meadows, rose petals.
   Set the hills to dancing,
Dress the canyon walls with live sheep,
   a drape of flax across the valleys.
Let them shout, and shout, and shout!
   Oh, oh, let them sing!

—Psalm 65:10–13

Probably the most unusual phrases in this psalm are "Drench the plowed fields, soak the dirt clods with rainfall as harrow and rake bring her to blossom and fruit." The psalmist's feeling is one of sheer abundance. He sees the year rising in the new life of spring as a queen crowned with the garlands of God, robed in the fresh new growth of the fields, and served by the flocks spread across hills and valleys. As we listen to the psalmist rhapsodize about these wonders, it would not be unusual to start wishing we were out there.

Although this psalm says nothing directly about it, the time in which it was written was filled with warnings about the man who would substitute nature for the church and do his worshipping there rather than in the ritual of the temple or church. The impulse is modernized in the man who says that he can worship God better looking at a beautiful sunset than praying some antique prayers in a stuffy church. He may worship better, but odds are that he is not worshipping God but rather the sun or, more probably, his own feeling about the sun.

The psalmist here is overwhelmed by God's gifts, but a danger looms that God's blessings or his creation might lure us away (see Romans 1:25). It's good to thank God for his provision; it's even better to seek him for who he is, regardless of our state of prosperity or want.

God's Forgiveness Unifies Our Lives

We all arrive at your doorstep sooner
   or later, loaded with guilt,
Our sins too much for us—
   but you get rid of them once and for all.

—Psalm 65:2-3

The history of Israel is a history of forgiveness. It is the story of the ignorant, the rebellious, the wicked, and the immature separating themselves from an original unity with God, and of him seeking them out and through forgiveness restoring them to that original unity again.

That story has its climax in Jesus Christ. The word *forgiveness* was often on his lips. In showing men the nature of God, he dramatically showed that forgiveness was God's primary intention toward man. There was to be a reconciliation between God and man. God was not far off in the heavens nurturing a grudge. Divinity was not a cold principle of retributive justice. The universe was not a mechanism set up to make sure that everyone got his just deserts. Instead, God sought man out to re-create him. He dealt with the wrongs of ignorance and immaturity and rebellion with eternal love. He worked in a unifying way to heal the terrible breach that had disorganized man and creation, brought incoherence into man's mind, and created a division between the spiritual and the physical.

God's forgiveness brings reconciliation. Whereas our lives naturally tend to unravel, God brings things together. His forgiveness brings us into relationship with him, with one another, and ultimately with all of his creation.

God Joins Us
in All of Life

I'm GOD, your God, the very God
   who rescued you from doom in Egypt,
Then fed you all you could eat,
   filled your hungry stomachs.

—Psalm 81:10

The common, always prevalent temptation is to separate our leisure, our entertainment, the light side of our lives, from God and his freedom-giving stance in our lives. But it is a malicious and devilish counsel—a counsel to eventual satiation, boredom, and eternal emptiness. The psalmist's message to us is that both our work and our pleasure can have a better, firmer source of action than the ones usually provided for us by cheap advertising and our own ephemeral dreams. The base for both work and play is in what happened back in Egypt: God's deliverance and gift of new life.

But there is something more to be said, something more personal and specific. In the midst of our songs and holiday festivals, we hear, as did Israel, the penetrating voice bringing the past into our present. And for us it is the voice of Christ: "Take my yoke upon you and learn from me. . . . For my yoke is easy and my burden is light" (Matthew 11:29–30, NIV). If Christ tells us anything, he tells us that escape from slavery does not mean exemption from labor. But what has happened is that he has joined us in the living of our lives, freed us from the slavery of brute circumstance and irrational sin, and welcomed us to the new, joyous work of sharing his ministry with him.

God's deliverance of the Hebrews from slavery in Egypt has a very real application to our lives today. Christ freed us from a meaningless, self-serving existence; then he invited us to share his ministry. Pay special attention to what his invitation means for your life.

God's Word Explains His Actions

I can't wait to hear what he'll say.
GOD's about to pronounce his people
well,
The holy people he loves so much,
so they'll never again live like fools.
See how close his salvation is to those who
fear him?
Our country is home base for Glory!

—Psalm 85:8-9

Here is the practical problem—the problem raised by our cynicism. How is what God speaks going to be any better than all the rest of the speaking? Isn't it just more words? The church says no and has some cogent reasoning to back it up. The Bible is the Word of God, but not just words.

God is a living God, active and involved in every part of the universe. He is Creator—the initiation and foundation of all things. He is Providence—sustaining and providing life for all things. He is Redeemer—recreating, salvaging, loving back to wholeness all that has rebelled and gone awry. This is all action, and because it is going on in history, which is in time and space that we can observe with our five senses, we can collect evidence for all this action. That is why Christianity places so much importance on history: it is the arena of the activity of God. But although history gives evidence of activity, not everyone agrees about what evidence means. Action is not more eloquent than words. Action, unexplained by the actor, can often be exceedingly confusing.

The Bible, the Word of God, brings this clarity, this articulation, this sense and solution out of the circumstantial evidence we have in the world of creation, providence, love, and goodness. The Word of God is the speaking side of the Action of God.

God's words reflect and, at times, foretell his actions. Likewise, his actions are clarified by his words. What are the words of God that have had a special impact on you recently? Can you identify his actions that are related to those words?

God Became Human to Elevate Us

Feature trumpets and big trombones,
Fill the air with praises to King GOD.

—Psalm 98:6

Soren Kierkegaard, the Danish theologian, tells a story that shows what God did in Jesus—the King, the Lord! There was once a king who lived high in a castle, enthroned in riches and power. In his regal passes through the village down below, he saw a little peasant girl with whom he fell in love. He fell so deeply in love with her that he wanted to marry her. He could have commanded her to be his wife, but it so happened that he really loved her and wanted her to love him, not just admire and respect his royal decree. His problem was to get her to respond to him in love and not to his riches, dignity, and honor. So he left the palace and disguised himself as a poor working peasant and went to live in the village, never revealing his royalty. He wooed the girl, won her love, and married her. And then, after he had won her simply by loving her, he took her back to the castle and put back on his robes and crown—and made her a queen. If he had come to her in all his splendor, he would have overwhelmed her and never reached her heart. Having reached her heart, he was able to elevate her to royalty and give her a crown and still have her love.

In this story, the king became a peasant in order to make a queen of a peasant girl, whom he loved. God in Christ became a common working man from an unremarkable region of Israel in order to welcome us into his kingdom. What is your response to the sacrificial love of God?

God Gives Us Life in Place of Death

I said to myself . . .
"Soul, you've been rescued from death;
Eye, you've been rescued from tears;
And you, Foot, were kept from stumbling."
I'm striding in the presence of GOD,
    alive in the land of the living!

—Psalm 116:8–9

One of the ways the Hebrew poets emphasized what they wanted to say was by putting two or three roughly synonymous statements one on top of the other. Here the psalmist parallels "Soul, you've been rescued from death" with "Eye, you've been rescued from tears" and "You, Foot, were kept from stumbling." In other words, a dead soul, tearful eyes, and stumbling feet are roughly synonymous. He is not talking about a man embalmed and ready to be dug into the ground; he is talking about himself in the state of biological life but existential death. A medical doctor would certify him alive, but he knows that he is already dead.

The reason the Hebrew could talk this way was because for him the basic fact of life was the reality of God. The Hebrew thought not as a biologist or physiologist but as a theologian. If God was not present and alive in a man's life, he was dead. The Hebrew author expressed this most forcibly in the story of Adam and Eve in the Garden of Eden. God had commanded them not to eat of a certain fruit from a certain tree, for if they did they would surely die. And then they ate it, and they died. But they didn't drop over dead. Yet the realm of death had invaded their existence.

The "land of the living" is the place where everything is in correspondence with its environment, living up to its created potential—that is, living openly toward God.

Is life without God merely breathing out of habit, existing but with nowhere to go? Think about his work of giving you life in place of death. Name ways he continues to give you the gift of life.

God Is Our Only Help

I look up to the mountains;
  does my strength come from mountains?
No, my strength comes from GOD,
  who made heaven, and earth, and
    mountains.

—Psalm 121:1–2

This psalm was written by the Hebrews in Israel for the occasion of the annual trek to Jerusalem. The annual festival at Jerusalem drew to it all who were able—whole families to worship God at the temple of Solomon. Jerusalem is located on a high mountain ridge, so from whatever direction one would approach it, that person would be traveling through hill country. Most of the pilgrims would be coming from the north, and that road would be in hill country all the way.

Now, in the first millennium BC, what did a man see when he lifted up his eyes to the hills? Baal worship. Baal, the Canaanite god, was worshipped on the hilltops. And every hill that amounted to anything in Palestine had a shrine to Baal that was frequented by the local populace. And the worship was a particularly vile kind, centering around cult prostitution and involving self-inflicted wounds.

The singers of the psalm lift up their eyes and ask, "Does my strength come from mountains? From these hills and what's going on there?" (see verse 1). And they answer with a resounding "No! Our help comes from God who made heaven, and earth, and mountains" (see verse 2).

If God had the power to create heaven and earth, he certainly has the power to restore what has been lost in your life. When you need help, don't look to a cheap substitute. God is your help.

We Were Created
for Lives of Faith

All you who fear GOD, how blessed you are!
how happily you walk on his smooth
straight road!

—Psalm 128:1

There is a general assumption prevalent in the world that it is extremely difficult to be a Christian. Many don't disqualify themselves completely, it is true, but they modify their claims— ordinary Christians, they call themselves. They respect the church, worship fairly regularly, try to live decently. But they also give themselves fairly generous margin to allow for the temptations and pressures put on them.

Actually, the easiest thing in the world is to be a Christian. What is hard is to be a sinner. Being a Christian is what we were created for. The life of faith has the support of an entire creation and the resources of a magnificent redemption. The structure of this world we live in was created by God so we could live in it easily and happily as his children. One of the things that happens in the way of Christian discipleship is the discovery that without Christ we were doing it the hard way and with Christ we are doing it the easy way. It is not the Christian who has it hard but the non-Christian.

How do you respond to the idea that God created the world in such a way that it supports a life of faith, making a life of sin by far the harder path to tread? How have you experienced God's creation augmenting your life of faith?

A Giver Receives
the Gift of Happiness

> Your wife will bear children as a vine bears
> grapes,
>   your household lush as a vineyard,
> The children around your table
>   as fresh and promising as young olive
>   shoots.
> Stand in awe of God's Yes.
>   Oh, how he blesses the one who fears
>   GOD!
>
> —Psalm 128:3-4

John Calvin, preaching to his congregation in Geneva, Switzerland, pointed out to his parishioners that we must develop better and deeper concepts of happiness than those held by the world, which makes a happy life to consist in ease, honors, and great wealth. Psalm 128 helps us do that. Too much of the world's happiness depends on taking from one to satisfy another. In order to increase my standard of living, someone in another part of the world must lower his. The worldwide crisis of hunger that we face today is a result of that method of pursuing happiness.

Industrialized nations acquire appetites for more and more luxuries and higher and higher standards of living, and increasing numbers of people are made poor and hungry. It doesn't have to be that way.

We have a greed problem—the widespread idea that if I don't grab mine while I can, I might not be happy. Christian blessing is a realization that "it is more blessed to give than to receive" (Acts 20:35, RSV). As we learn to give and to share, our vitality increases, and the people around us become "fruitful vines" (see Psalm 128:3, RSV) and "olive shoots" around our tables.

Think of a time when you shared generously with another person. You gave freely, not out of obligation or under duress. What did giving things away, in contrast to grasping things, do for your life?

God Made Us for Community

How wonderful, how beautiful,
    when brothers and sisters get along!
It's like costly anointing oil
    flowing down head and beard,
Flowing down Aaron's beard,
    flowing down the collar of his priestly
      robes.

—Psalm 133:1–2

The roots of our faith community reach back into Israel, where we find, always, that the congregation was the basic working unit in God's relationships with his people. In the Hebrew legal system, to be cut off from the community was the worst punishment. An individual forced to live in exile was not a whole person. There are no Robinson Crusoe traditions in the biblical narrative. You can be damned by yourself, but you cannot be saved by yourself. And it follows that no work of ministry is possible apart from community.

We who live in communities of faith and work for the building up of families of faith attract a lot of interest, for individualism hasn't worked. The cult of self-sufficiency hasn't sufficed. Persons are wistful for intimacy. But nothing we do is more difficult. The only way I know to renew and deepen my participation in the community of faith is to immerse myself in the source materials of the people of God—the original and formative experiences that brought this family into being. Psalm 133 is one that has made a difference for me.

Western culture honors the rugged individualist, the lone wolf, the type A, steamroller-style leader. It was just the opposite for the Hebrews. How can we overcome current cultural values to minister within "the basic working unit in God's relationships with his people"?

Nothing Is Unimportant to God

Lady Wisdom goes out in the street and
    shouts.
    At the town center she makes her speech.
In the middle of the traffic she takes her
    stand.
    At the busiest corner she calls out.

—Proverbs 1:20–21

E ven our so-called secular lives are permeated by grace; even the nonreligious aspects of our lives are included in the Bible. The Word of God to us is not only the radical invasion into our lives by Christ, not only that tremendous life-changing reconciliation that puts us in relationship with the Eternal Being, but also a detailed concern with our humanity. The gospel is not just a statement about the big issues and the deep realities; it is also about the time of day and the feeling you have when you get up in the morning.

Proverbs is the biblical statement that everything—including ants, spouses, overeating, compliments, curiosity—every detail of life is of infinite, eternal importance. Loneliness is as important a reality as divine love. The factory is as high on the agenda as is faith. Family life is discussed with the same seriousness as the life of the Godhead. The words of men are ranged along the words of God for examination. Nothing is excluded from life; everything is included. Proverbs puts into Scripture all those details that we might suppose are of no importance to God and unaffected by grace.

Have you ever avoided praying about something because you felt God would never be interested in such a "small" matter? How does his all-encompassing wisdom from the book of Proverbs encourage you to bring *everything* before him?

Gossip and Hurry Are Our Enemies

Keep vigilant watch over your heart;
that's where life starts.

—Proverbs 4:23

There were two heart-enemies that the wise men in Israel were particularly alert to, and their vigilance in regard to them continues to be helpful to us. The enemies were hurry and gossip. Hurry is the pathological form of action. Gossip is the degenerative form of speech.

An important way to guard our hearts against hurry is to engage in worship. Worship is the place where we are purged from hurry so that we can act in simple effectiveness. We find out what God is doing and hear what he commands us to do. And suddenly the panicky hustle is taken out of our work. Our energies are focused and become useful.

Speech is evidence of intelligence, meaning, and dignity. But very often it is evidence of stupidity, triviality, and nonsense. When speech is used in the form of gossip, it betrays its nature. The most important protection of the authenticity of speech is the Bible. It is difficult to read, but not because it is highly intellectual or mystically complex. The difficulty is that we are not used to honest, direct, and personal speech. But we read it anyway and in the process find our hearts addressed cleanly. We read it, listening and praying, and find our hearts strangely warmed.

Speech is intended to convey intelligence, meaning, and dignity. What does gossip convey? And living in a hurry works against "simple effectiveness." The remedy is the worship of God. Have you found that to be true? Why or why not?

Wisdom Brings Harmony

GOD sovereignly made me—the first,
        the basic—
    before he did anything else. . . .
And then staked out Earth's Foundations,
    I was right there with him, making sure
            everything fit.
Day after day I was there, with my joyful
        applause,
    always enjoying his company,
Delighted with the world of things and
        creatures,
    happily celebrating the human family.

—Proverbs 8:22, 29–31

I n the last part of this proverb, there is this sentence: "Day after day I was there, with my joyful applause, always enjoying his company." The RSV translates that last phrase as "like a master work-man." God creates. Christ redeems. But then what? We have this magnificent creation; we have this great salvation. But who is going to build them into the individual personal history that is you? That is wisdom's task. Wisdom is God's master workman. God assigns himself to fashion in you an individual history including all your days, all your environment, all your circumstances—a life lived to his glory in which you enjoy him forever.

When the Greek translators got to this term—*master workman*—they translated it with their word *harmodzousa,* "the harmonizer." We know what harmony is. Imagine a piano in a house. At times, a child visits and sits before it and bangs on the keys. That is not music, though; that is noise. But another visitor arrives who goes to the keyboard and, using exactly the same keys, provides the household with delight. The same notes are struck, but they are played harmoniously. The master workman is the harmonizer. Wisdom is the harmonizer. The Holy Spirit is the harmonizer.

How would you describe times when your life has lacked harmony? What was it that restored the harmony you were missing? Looking back, do you now see wisdom at work in this process?

Wisdom Is Life

Come with me, oh come, have
dinner with me!
I've prepared a wonderful spread—
fresh-baked bread,
roast lamb, carefully selected wines.
Leave your impoverished confusion
and *live*!
Walk up the street to a life with
meaning.

—Proverbs 9:5–6

A major task of Wisdom is simply to get herself taken seriously. At a key place in the Proverbs, we find the problem dealt with in the form of a dramatization, a kind of skit between two women: a wise woman and a foolish woman. They are competing for the attention of the people on the street. Both women stand on high places in the city and invite with these words: "Leave your impoverished confusion and *live*!" In this context, "impoverished confusion" doesn't mean simplemindedness but rather open-mindedness. The verbal form of the word means to be spacious, be wide, be open. The invitation, then, is to those who are eager for instruction, who are ready to be taught, who are conscious of their ignorance and naïveté, who are aware of their inability to carry on the business of life and want some help and training.

Wisdom's atmosphere is open, free, joyful. It is all out in the open, celebrative and expansive. The atmosphere of foolishness is not so much an invitation as it is a seduction: "Steal off with me, I'll show you a good time!" (verse 17). Her offerings are shrouded in lies. It makes a difference how you live. It makes a difference whose advice you listen to. It makes a difference whose counsel you take. This is the difference between life and death.

How do you discern the difference between wisdom and foolishness? Both teach lessons, but only the lessons of wisdom lead to life. How do you define *life* in this context?

The Family Is a
Place of Healing

Exploit or abuse your family, and end up
with a fistful of air;
common sense tells you it's a stupid way
to live.

—Proverbs 11:29

K nowing this, and seeing it confirmed to our observing eyes
day after day in both our own families and those around
us, it is an easy game to predict dire destinies for all who trouble
their households. Many today are playing the game: sociologists,
psychiatrists, and critics of the home and family. But it does little
good to predict that we will inherit the wind when the wind is already howling down upon us. In the face of this, we find Proverbs
least helpful. We need more than warnings; we need help.

We need to step back from this proverb and see who said it
and the whole area of concern. It is spoken by a Hebrew wise man
to a community of faith that was Israel and that has since become
the church. And this context of conversation provides much more

than just the threat of what will happen if we behave badly. It also provides the antidote to our troubles. That is to say, the family is not only the unit in which we see disaster, but it is also the unit in which divine love can be and is perfected. The positive thing the biblical message has to say is this: when we begin to inherit the wind, the solution is not to flee but to stay. The family is precisely the place where healing may be discovered, where new life can emerge, and where calm may be restored by God's grace.

"The family is not only the unit in which we see disaster, but it is also the unit in which divine love can be and is perfected." Few people would say that life in a family is easy. However, it can teach us about God and about ourselves. Can you give an example of this?

God Calls Us to Be Healers

A cheerful disposition is good for your
health;
gloom and doom leave you bone-tired.

—Proverbs 17:22

D on't misunderstand. The claim is not that if you have perfect joy and tell a lot of uproarious jokes, your body will be
perfectly healthy. This is no promise that if you just think the right
way, everything will be heavenly. There is a religious sect (Christian Scientism) that teaches that, but it must deny the reality of all
material and bodily evidence to do it. The church does not make
that presumption. Scripture does not support the extreme position,
and neither does our experience—experience such as the man in
trouble being told, "Cheer up. Things could get worse." He cheered
up, and sure enough, things did get worse.

The position is rather this: we are created as whole persons by
God with a body and a mind that have deep and complex effects
on each other. This works both ways, of course. Pain in the body af-
fects the thoughts of the mind and the feelings of the heart. Bodily
healing, for that reason, has always had a lot of attention from the

church. The good Samaritan who bound up the wounds of the man who had fallen among thieves didn't quote the proverb "A cheerful disposition is good for your health." No, rather he poured in oil and wine and dealt with his suffering.

Helping to bring healing calls for effective action, not simply giving advice. There is nothing wrong with discussing the best ways to alleviate suffering, but suffering will continue until someone takes action. What approaches have done the most to help you in times of suffering?

The Intimacy
of Teaching Others

Point your kids in the right direction—
when they're old they won't be lost.

—Proverbs 22:6

The oft-heard phrase is *train up*. In this verse it is rendered *point,* but either way, it is very important. It is the only time in the entire Old Testament that it is used just this way. Literally, the word means to rub the palate of a newborn child with oil before it begins to nurse—a practice used by midwives in the ancient east. The word then broadened out to describe what you do to infants and children to get them started right in life. The phrase was later used for things—for houses and temples—and the act you performed to get them started right: in essence, a dedication. One of the famous feasts of the Jews is called Chanukah, the feast of dedication.

Train up has to me, at least, an impersonal sound—the kind of thing you do with animals to make them useful and obedient. But *hanakh,* the initial word in this famous proverb, has warmth and intimacy to it. The midwife who rubs the gums of an infant to prepare her for the breast is acting in a warm, caring way, the purpose of which is to initiate the infant into a living activity. Any Christian who thinks he can train up another into the Christian faith by drawing some maps, compiling some statistics, and painting some pictures is going to end up in a place of extreme disappointment. That's not the way it works.

Teaching others is not an arm's-length enterprise. It calls for personal engagement. Think of the teacher (or mentor, coach, or other person) whose influence continues to affect you. What are the leading characteristics of that person's investment in your life?

We Grow in Relationship to Others

You use steel to sharpen steel,
and one friend sharpens another.

—Proverbs 27:17

Not to be sharp is to be dull. And we have enough of that kind of experience, both in others and in ourselves. Our minds, feelings, and responses often seem to be blunted and dull. We know we are not getting everything we can out of life. But if we find ourselves dull, how do we get sharp? How do we achieve our best as persons? How do we become all that we can be?

We do it in personal relationships. One person encounters another. There is interchange of feelings. There is dialogue. We are complex, profound, amazing creatures, and we must function in the society of other persons if we are to develop to our maximum potentials. Our bodies can be developed through exercise, our minds can be developed through thinking, our appearance can be developed through decoration. But we—the whole self, the ego, the me—find ourselves and develop only in relation with another person. That is the sole way to sharpen.

One might say that living in isolation is a dull experience, or perhaps a dulled experience. Sharpening comes in relationship with other people. Name five ways you have found your life to be richer and more complete as a result of being in close relationship with others.

God's View of Women Breaks Barriers

A good woman is hard to find,
  and worth far more than diamonds.
Her husband trusts her without reserve,
  and never has reason to regret it.

—Proverbs 31:10–11

Even a superficial examination of the ancient world—and in some ways it isn't much different than the modern world—shows the two stereotypes of woman: either she is a centerfold seductress, or she is a household drudge, a sexy siren or a humble hausfrau. In that context we arrive at Proverbs 31. The description of woman completely steps outside those stereotypes and gives an original insight into what it means to be a woman. There is not a line in this description about woman being subject to man, either as his inferior or his temptress. It is rather a picture of a person who is intelligent, confident, respected and honored, involved in community and humanitarian work, capable of initiative, trustworthy, and creative.

Do you see the power of this third option? If you are a woman, it is a liberating picture to be something you might not have thought possible. And if you are a man, it frees you to relate to a woman as a person in her own right. This is not propaganda; this is the gospel. This is not part of a debate on the role of women in society; it is a declaration of good news about who we all are.

Human categories lack the wideness of God's freeing description of our identity. Man-made descriptions of people lack dimension and serve to limit us. But when God looks at us, we are invited into a bigger life. Put into words what he sees when he looks at you.

Everything Is
Part of God's Time

There's an opportune time to do things, a right
time for everything on the earth:
      A right time for birth and another for
            death,
      A right time to plant and another to reap,
      A right time to kill and another to heal,
      A right time to destroy and another to
            construct,
      A right time to cry and another to laugh.

—Ecclesiastes 3:1–4

This vibrant, poetic passage from the center of Ecclesiastes shows what looks to be opposite: birth, death, weeping, dancing, planting, plucking, breaking down, and building up. However, instead of contrasting them, these verses incorporate them. They are not opposites in life that contradict each other but rather realities of life that God puts together. There is a time for this and a time for that. They are not the same thing, but they are included in God's time. Everything that happens, in other words, is part of God's time. No matter what happens, the scripture says, it's the right time.

Two things we commonly exclude from the good times are suffering and work. But both are things that we all have to face. When we are suffering, we keep hoping for the time of health when we are not suffering. When we are working, we are looking for that time of leisure when we are not working and can enjoy ourselves. The verses here say that is a mistake. If you pursue that way of thinking, you are missing out, missing great opportunities of God's presence with you. You are leaving him out of some very significant parts of your life, and you are losing what he has in store for you at those times.

When we exclude hard times from the category of things we value, we miss "great opportunities of God's presence." Look back to such a time in your life. Did you realize later on that you had missed a meaningful time with God?

When Faith Becomes Institutionalized

Watch your step when you enter God's
   house.
  Enter to learn. That's far better than mind-
     lessly offering a sacrifice,
  Doing more harm than good.
Don't shoot off your mouth, or speak before
     you think.
Don't be too quick to tell God what you think
     he wants to hear.
God's in charge, not you—the less you speak,
     the better.

—Ecclesiastes 5:1–2

I t is dangerous to go to church. Be on your guard when you
get near a church, for there are some terrible things that can
happen to you there. It is like walking on a glacier: dangerous cre-
vasses threaten your life. It is like driving a car: there are numerous
dangers when you get behind the wheel. The dangers do not mean
you shouldn't climb or drive but rather that you must be extremely
careful.

When we enter the realm of the Christian religion, we open ourselves to an existence characterized by God speaking to us, promising to order our lives and love and redeem us in his mercy. The danger is that as we get together in the name of God, we will merely chatter with each other about our morals and our meetings and drown out his voice. The danger is that we will get so busy running a religious institution that we have no energy or attention left over for a personal encounter with a personal God. The danger is that we treat the whole business of religion as something we are in charge of, that we must plan, administer, and complete. This is what Ecclesiastes calls "the sacrifice of fools" (verse 1, RSV), or what I refer to as religion in the wrong place.

What effect do planning and budget meetings and the work of the buildings and grounds committee have on your faith? How have you felt you might be in danger of viewing your life of faith as something that furthers the success of an institution?

We Alone Can Accept God-Given Joy

Seize life! Eat bread with gusto,
Drink wine with a robust heart.
Oh yes—God takes pleasure in
your pleasure!
Dress festively every morning.
Don't skimp on colors and scarves.

—Ecclesiastes 9:7-8

Ecclesiastes is in Scripture to help strip us of illusions and sentimentality—those things in life that, while good in themselves, pose as something high and mighty and divert us from God. And one of those areas where we need help is in the pursuit of pleasure. There is no way to have an experience of God without also having an experience of joy. But we must not suppose that Ecclesiastes is going to instruct us in right and wrong pleasures. This is not his style. His question is not "What is right?" but "What is real?" He summarizes the mistake we make in regard to God's joy in two statements.

First, we must not pursue pleasure, for it is a gift to be enjoyed, not a goal to be pursued. The pursuit of pleasure leads to a swamp of boredom. No one is more insistent than Ecclesiastes that we enjoy life while at the same time warning of the danger of investing those enjoyments with a life of their own. Second, we cannot purchase pleasure. Joys are given by God; man can only accept them. We cannot create them, earn them, or hoard and accumulate them. In our world every commonplace novelty is breathlessly proclaimed as an original creation that we can acquire by purchase. But joys cannot be bought, only received. The one thing we can do to develop a capacity for enjoyment is to practice generosity—a kind of reckless sharing that imitates the divine largesse.

God is the supreme Joy Giver, the one legitimate Source of joy. Have you ever devoted yourself to the pursuit of joy, only to end up feeling depleted and cheated? "Joys cannot be bought, only received." Look to God for joy.

We Are Made to Live in Love

Love is invincible facing danger and death.
Passion laughs at the terrors of hell.
The fire of love stops at nothing—
it sweeps everything before it.

—Song of Solomon 8:7

What is a book like this doing in the Bible? The name of God is nowhere to be found, even by inference. There is nothing about worship, morals, sin, or forgiveness. It is easy to understand why love poetry is written, but how does it come to be in holy Scripture? What is the meaning of the church's belief that this is the Word of God?

It means that we were created physically, emotionally, and mentally to live in love. It's very easy to lose sight of this because we have so much trouble with the intimacy and faithfulness that love requires. Our experience is so unhappy and we do such a poor job of it, so why talk about it anymore? Despite our sordid failures in love, we see here what we are created for, what God intends for us.

The other thing meant by the presence of the Song of Solomon in our Bibles is that all love is sacramental. To be sacramental means that it is a sign of the holy. The physical is a container of the spiritual, the visible is evidence of the invisible, the profane a conduit for the religious. Human love, sacramentally, is the arena in which we learn the meaning of love and thus of God's love. Jesus Christ, in order to show us the love of God, took the form of a man and loved particular persons in actual history. Now it is our turn to engage in acts of love that are a pattern of the divine love.

How often does love fit God's pattern? Or to put it differently, before we seek to act in love, how often do we first look to his pattern? Think of an example that contrasts God's pattern for living in love (see Lamentations 3:22) with the love that disappoints us.

God Sees Our Competencies Clearly

GOD told me, "Don't say, 'I'm only a boy.'
I'll tell you where to go and you'll go
there.
I'll tell you what to say and you'll say it."

—Jeremiah 1:7

In the really important things of life, we are terrifyingly unqualified. And if we don't know it, we are in for a lot of trouble. We are inadequate as parents, we are inadequate as spouses, and we are inadequate as friends. Most of all we're inadequate as Christians. And then around the periphery of these core elements of incompetency as human beings, there are many other instances that remind us of our lack of know-how. But the piece of wrong thinking that fuels these inadequacies is that we think of ourselves in terms of roles or functions or positions or performance. Jeremiah disqualifies himself on the basis of his role, his status: he is young and inexperienced with not the faintest idea of what to do.

But here is the surprise. God dismisses Jeremiah's disclaimer, which is to say, "Jeremiah, forget about what you think about yourself or what the neighbors think of you, how old you are or whether you are a potter or stonemason or teacher. I am in charge here, I'm giving the orders, I am telling you where to go, I am going with you, and if you get into trouble, I will rescue you. I am the ground for your life, your work, who you are and what you do. I am the reality who determines your reality."

Only God has complete knowledge of who you are. If he says you are qualified, you are qualified. If he chooses you for a task, he isn't making a mistake. You have known yourself since you were a baby; God has known you since before the beginning of time.

The Thankless Task of Helping Others

You pushed me into this, GOD,
    and I let you do it.
    You were too much for me.
And now I'm a public joke.
    They all poke fun at me.
Every time I open my mouth
    I'm shouting, "Murder!" or "Rape!
And all I get for my GOD-warnings
    are insults and contempt.

—Jeremiah 20:7–8

Having the choice between a smile and a frown, who wouldn't choose the smile? It brightens the landscape. It lifts the spirits. So it's kind of a shock to meet up with the prophet Jeremiah. He didn't have a happy face. He was the kind of person others laughed at, and the experience wasn't pleasant: "I'm a public joke." If a man is really right with God and doing God's work, shouldn't he be happy?

Jeremiah preached in and around Jerusalem for over twenty-five years at the end of the seventh century BC. It was a time when the nation was threatened by the rising Babylonian Empire. Jeremiah did his best to get the people to take seriously God's will for the nation and make plain to them the judgment that would come upon them if they persisted in defying his laws. God called Jeremiah to be his spokesman, but every time he spoke, the words that came out were offensive to the people. On the other hand, if he tried to be quiet, he could not hold it in. He couldn't keep quiet, and he couldn't speak anything that people were pleased to hear. He couldn't live with himself if he was silent, and he couldn't live with his countrymen if he spoke. The intensity of his suffering angrily burst out in the violent complaint "Cursed be the day on which I was born!" (verse 14, RSV).

Jeremiah obeyed God by issuing warnings of coming doom. He said of his work, "I'm shouting, 'Murder!' or 'Rape!'" (verse 8). It's no wonder he wasn't a favorite party guest. Think of your recent attempts to help someone. How often was the process a pleasure?

How God's Unfairness Saves Us

This is the brand-new covenant that I will make with Israel when the time comes. I will put my law within them—write it on their hearts!—and be their God. And they will be my people.

—Jeremiah 31:33

We are the people who have known such a covenant and have broken such a covenant. Jeremiah brings us the word of God's new covenant, and without exaggeration, it is absolutely staggering. Why? Because it is unexpected. God has made a covenant with man, and man has broken this covenant. There are established ways man can fix this; it is his responsibility, his job. But then God speaks—he takes the initiative again! God, who with absolute justice could have left the responsibility with man, has graciously started over again.

The sovereign God asserts his power and authority and deals with the deepest wrong in our lives. There is no frivolous, superficial rearranging of symptoms and feelings but a deep, radical salvation of our central being: the forgiveness of our sins.

The further staggering thing is not that these things can be done, or even that God will do them, but that he will do them again, that he will establish a new covenant. And in that newness the meaning is intensified in internalization, in experience, and in ultimacy.

Forgiveness is not fair. Think of a time when you needed to forgive someone who had betrayed you and you resisted. Is it fair that the wronged party has to forgive? Yet it is God's nature to keep forgiving humanity, which continues to betray him.

When Common Sins Get Free Passes

"Come. Sit down. Let's argue this
    out."
  This is GOD's Message:
"If your sins are blood-red,
    they'll be snow-white.
If they're red like crimson,
    they'll be like wool."

—Isaiah 1:18

It is clear right off that Isaiah is for getting rid of sin altogether—wiping it out. But there are people (and great philosophers are numbered among them) who think that sin is useful in setting off the picture of life by providing shadows and backgrounds. Light would be very monotonous if unrelieved by any contrasting shadows. There is a certain plausibility to all of this, so Isaiah's radical stand is a little surprising in a way. Why is he so stiff-necked about sin? Is he just an incurable Puritan? Hardly. His unreasonable opposition to sin springs rather from his sensitivity and love for his nation, Israel.

Israel was sick from sin. That nation as a whole was on its last legs. To the average man on the street in Israel, none of it looked too bad. He wasn't sick, wasn't riddled with anxiety, wasn't guilty about temple superficiality, and hardly knew any orphans or widows. The same could be said for many of us: the world's not great, but it's not so bad, either. And so we are the ones Isaiah is calling to sit down and think about our sins—the sins we moderately and rather thoughtlessly indulge. And what he means by being reasonable about our sins is to get rid of them altogether, to wipe them out.

Sin violates God's will for us. And when life is comfortable, it can be more difficult to notice the work of sin. While Isaiah denounces sin in the harshest terms, he doesn't fail to remind us of God's nature, which is to get rid of sin altogether.

What a Covenant
Means to God

Can you think of anything I could have done
to my vineyard that I didn't do?
When I expected good grapes,
why did I get bitter grapes?

—Isaiah 5:4

Once upon a time there was an atheist climbing a mountain. At a very high altitude on a very dangerous slope, he slipped, stumbled over the edge of a sheer cliff, and desperately grabbed at the cliff edge and held on. There was no help around, and his fingers began to get tired. Dangling thousands of feet over a rocky chasm, he finally cried out, "O God, if there is a God, I will do anything. Just save me." He repeated the prayer several times when suddenly he was interrupted by a thundering voice. "Do you really mean anything?" The atheist said, "Anything!" The voice then said, "Okay, let go." The atheist replied indignantly, "Are you kidding?"

Once upon a time there was a nation highly skilled in religion. They had a lot of experience and a great reputation for knowing where they were in relation to God. They were called God's chosen people. Then they had an accident: they slipped and fell as a nation, left hanging by their fingertips. They were about to be destroyed by a conquering army when they called out to God, "Save us. We'll do anything. Just don't let us be destroyed." The voice of God thundered, "Anything?" The nation said, "Anything, but be quick about it." God said, "Okay, love your neighbor." And the nation said, "Are you kidding?"

What more could God do? He created a nation by making a promise to an aged man and woman. Their descendants in faith have been a mixed lot at best, but God has never disowned them. How would you describe his repeated refusal to give up on his people?

God's Gracious Way of Invading Our World

The people who walked in darkness
   have seen a great light.
For those who lived in a land of deep
      shadows—
   light! sunbursts of light! . . .
For a child has been born—for us!

—Isaiah 9:2, 6

The fact that this divine invasion took place through the birth of a baby is a very significant feature of the narrative. God could have visited us any way he chose. But this is the way he chose. For us it appears to be the most gracious, the most polite (if we can use that word of God) way in which it could have been done, for we are not suddenly confronted with deity but led to divinity through humanity. "For to us a child is born" (verse 6, RSV), and we learn to love this son. We are thrilled at his birth, live with him to his maturity, admire and are challenged by him in his adult ministry, and (if we continue this association with him) are finally led to say with Peter, "You are the Christ, the Son of the living

God" (Matthew 16:16, RSV). He began as our son, and he emerges as God's Son, sent to save us from our sins.

Emmanuel, God with us, is not something that is set up to shock us or provide a theological spectator thrill. It is designed rather to effectively and surely lead us from the natural to the supernatural, from the human to the divine, from the son given to us to God's Son given for us.

God didn't use the temple mount to announce his invasion of human life; instead, he chose an unremarkable site smelling of animal dung. He didn't send a heavily armed warrior; he sent a helpless newborn. God's modus operandi is described as "gracious" and "polite." How would you describe the Incarnation?

God's Coming Salvation

> Energize the limp hands,
>   strengthen the rubbery knees.
> Tell fearful souls,
>   "Courage! Take heart!
> GOD is here, right here,
>   on his way to put things right
> And redress all wrongs.
>   He's on his way! He'll save you!"

> —Isaiah 35:3–4

Every tragedy that we experience will, finally, become a triumph. Every deficiency in our ability to see or hear or walk or speak will be cured by grace. Everything in our bodies that does not work will, finally, be made workable to the glory of God. Everything in our souls that does not respond to the will of God will become, through the power of forgiveness and the ministrations of mercy, an instrument of God's peace. The wholeness will be achieved on every level: material, physical, spiritual, personal, social. Jesus, by healing the blind and deaf and dumb and lame, made sure we would not misinterpret Isaiah 35 by spiritualizing it, making poetic figures of it to symbolize defects in our character.

And Jesus, by not healing all the blind and deaf and dumb and lame, also made sure we would not misinterpret Isaiah 35 by secularizing it, shortcutting God's purposes by trying to fix in our own strength all that ails the world. The wholeness will be the wholeness of the entire creation brought to a redeemed finish. Every hour of every day we live is a word or sentence or paragraph of the story that will finally come to this conclusion.

God knows the end from before the beginning. His promises are trustworthy but not always to be fulfilled in our lifetimes. Still, his salvation, his healing, and his faithfulness to his Word can be counted on for eternity. How do you respond to such a God?

Leaders Should Beware the Justice of God

I myself will be the shepherd of my sheep. I myself will make sure they get plenty of rest. I'll go after the lost, I'll collect the strays, I'll doctor the injured, I'll build up the weak ones and oversee the strong ones so they're not exploited.

—Ezekiel 34:15–16

I don't find anywhere where Jesus quoted from Ezekiel 34. But there are several places where he says things that show he has meditated on Ezekiel long enough that the imagery and message have gotten into his bones. A piece of writing that was so important to Jesus simply has to have something important for us.

A sense of compassion permeates this material. Ezekiel looks at his countrymen and sees them as people who have been treated badly, exploited, and used by others. And he is angry about that. God, using Ezekiel as his spokesman, erupts with hot anger over what is happening among the human beings he has created to live in a very different way. But there is more than anger here—there is responsibility.

God sets out to do himself what needs to be done for the people he creates and loves. There has been a disastrous failure in leadership. Though it was his original plan that men should exercise leadership that would express love and justice, it simply isn't happening. So God takes the initiative. He will shepherd himself, taking care of the unfortunate and the weak and exercising a careful rule over "the fat and the strong" (verse 16, RSV).

Long before Jesus unleashed his harshest words against Pharisees and teachers of the Law, Ezekiel announced God's judgment on "the fat and the strong." Human ambition seeks status and prosperity. But every leader who rejects God's way of mercy and healing should anticipate his judgment.

Ezekiel Saw God's Work in Advance

God said to me, "Son of man, these bones are the whole house of Israel. Listen to what they're saying: 'Our bones are dried up, our hope is gone, there's nothing left of us.'

"Therefore, prophesy. Tell them, 'GOD, the Master, says: I'll dig up your graves and bring you out alive—O my people! Then I'll take you straight to the land of Israel.

—Ezekiel 37:11-12

Ezekiel was a seer, a visionary. It is the best thing about him and that which makes him a giant in the way of faith. He saw beneath the surface of things and into the reality. Ezekiel was a pastor to people who were alone and homeless, who felt dismembered, dried up, and cut off from the living fountain of faith. Hope was missing, and they felt like dry bones. What could be said to people like that? What could be done for them?

God spoke through Ezekiel. And what he had already seen in his vision began to happen with the people with whom he lived.

His words linked the reality of the vision to their everyday lives. Ezekiel painted a picture of God's reality that no one could see because they were too busy feeling sorry for themselves. He told them what he saw, and then they began to see it and participate in it. They began to respond to what God was doing instead of what they were feeling. They began to live by God's words instead of the gossip of their neighbors. They began to walk by faith, not by sight.

Ezekiel was human like the rest of us, but he could see God's reality beyond the surface of human experience. He led God's people to live by faith, not by sight. Whom do you know who faithfully speaks the reality of God, even when it goes against the grain of human assumptions?

God's Mercy and Natural Consequences

> Because of the three great sins of Israel
> —make that four—I'm not putting up
> with them any longer.
> They buy and sell upstanding people.
> People for them are only *things*—ways of
> making money.
> They'd sell a poor man for a pair of shoes.
> They'd sell their own grandmother!
> They grind the penniless into the dirt,
> shove the luckless into the ditch.
> Everyone and his brother sleeps with the
> "sacred whore"—
> a sacrilege against my Holy Name.
>
> —Amos 2:6-7

We find nothing in Amos of what is abundant in other prophets—nothing of mercy, nothing of grace, nothing of steadfast love. There is no compassion, no attempt to understand the circumstances, no appreciation for the difficulty of their lives. He holds out no hope for a better future and shows no understanding of the mixture of motives at work in all of us, no appreciation of the tragic aspects of life. He says one thing with poetic genius and prophetic courage and moral passion: God's judgment is about to be visited on the people.

It is not a very pretty picture, nor is it an unusual picture. The Hebrew society that Amos confronts has alarming parallels to our society today. Then, as now, God will not put up with it. Judgment is coming. God will make no exceptions. The prophet's words hammer away, penetrating the thick defenses of excuse making and rationalization. Amos uses every picture he can paint, every memory he can revive, every terror he can imagine in order to warn the people, to prepare them for judgment.

God's tireless mercy does not set aside the consequences of our actions. The Hebrew society of Amos's day presents "alarming parallels" to our society. What are the beginnings of God's judgment on our nation?

God Is Not a Celestial Robot

> Why can't I likewise change what I feel about
> Nineveh from anger to pleasure, this big
> city of more than 120,000 childlike people
> who don't yet know right from wrong, to say
> nothing of all the innocent animals?
>
> —Jonah 4:11

God is not a stolid, immovable principle of being. He has not set up mechanical laws of human existence that are going to be carried out impersonally and fatalistically. The universe he created is full of possibility, full of freedom, full of surprise. He is alive in all of this—changing, responding, redeeming, working continuously in it. This is why all fixed, mechanical concepts of predestination are foreign to the spirit of Scripture. God has not ordered the details of your life so that they will come to pass willy-nilly regardless of what you do. You are a person, and God respects you as such. You can change—respond, initiate, create. As you do, God—who is always living in personal reaction and present grace—changes, responds, initiates, and creates.

When we talk of God repenting, we are not suggesting that he made a mistake and is sorry he made it and is now going to start over again. We are saying that God changes, moves with the situation, redeems what has gone wrong. If 120,000 Ninevites change their way of life, God changes his tactics in response to them. He is not bound to a pattern. He is not committed to a blueprint. If men and women respond in new ways to his presence, he will respond in creative new ways to them.

God created the universe as a place of relationship. This rules out a mechanistic existence in which the Creator established the rules and then backed away. Recall a time when God responded to human obedience, initiative, or faithful living.

The Offended
Initiates Forgiveness

You're our last hope. Is it not true
that in you the orphan finds mercy?

—Hosea 14:3

Hosea was a prophet. As such, he preached a creative, new word. It had, and continues to have, the penetrating, incisory characteristics of a sharp sword. The word he preached was that of forgiveness. As one reads the prophecy of Hosea, a couple of grand truths about forgiveness jump off the page with astonishing force and brilliance. The first is that forgiveness is learned by forgiving. It was the crucial act in the life of Hosea. The forgiveness that Hosea gave Gomer provided the knowledge, experience, and initiative for him to fulfill his calling as the great preacher of God's forgiveness to Israel.

Another truth is that there is a strategy behind forgiveness. The folklore on forgiveness is that the offender is to seek it, to say "I'm sorry; forgive me." If we are generous and goodwilled, we can then forgive. But the initiative must come from the one seeking forgiveness. The biblical statement is the other way around. God the offended makes the first move and continues with unrelenting effort to get us to accept his forgiveness. The truth is dual: we must accept the forgiveness so quickly and steadfastly offered to us by God, and we must initiate forgiveness among those who are in our debt, the "our debtors" (Matthew 6:12, RSV) of the Lord's Prayer. Forgiveness is deepest when it is initiated and planned by the offended. That is why Christ being crucified on a cross offering forgiveness is the most powerful image of forgiveness we have.

Hosea the prophet married a prostitute who continued to ply her trade. Hosea continued to accept her back, finally buying his unfaithful wife to save her from the sex trade. God's forgiveness of his unfaithful people is unrelenting. What is your response?

CONCLUSION

And there you have it. Ninety days of walking through a handful of Old Testament books alongside the mind and pen of Eugene Peterson. Our hope is that every day or every step was an arrival of God's truth specific to your life and circumstances, in the form of encouragement or challenge or possibly even conviction. There was no predetermined concluding place as we curated these entries, no landfall we had to make by the last day. We did not begin with an end in mind, so to speak. The days just sort of fell into place.

So you can imagine our surprise and delight when the heart of Day 90's entry was a beautiful and humbling reminder of God's unrelenting mercy. It felt *true, noble, reputable, authentic, compelling,* and *gracious* (Philippians 4:8). Again, we did not plan it that way. That was something beyond our hands.

The final four words of this devotional collection arrived in the form of a question: *What is your response?* That feels like a good foot to both finish and then begin again on. What was and will be your response to the arrivals you've experienced over the last ninety days? There is by no means just one. In fact, it's more likely you've witnessed a number of feelings and impressions and memories and hopes. Test them. Try them. Trust them.

Our prayer is that as you reflect on them you will see a discernible thread sewn through each, the tie that indeed binds this all together—the unrelenting mercy of God. Amen.

WaterBrook and Multnomah Editorial Team